Western Journeys

Western Journeys

TEOW LIM GOH

THE UNIVERSITY OF UTAH PRESS
Salt Lake City

The Defiance House Man colophon is a registered trademark of the University of Utah Press. It is based on a four-foot-tall Ancient Puebloan pictograph (late PIII) near Glen Canyon, Utah.

ISBN 978-1-64769-096-0 (paperback)
ISBN 978-1-64769-095-3 (ebook)

Catalog-in-Publication data for this title is available online at the Library of Congress.

Errata and further information on this and other titles available online at UofUpress.com.

Printed and bound in the United States of America.

Contents

I
Beyond the Myths

Hollywood Pilgrims

I RECOGNIZED MONUMENT VALLEY long before I saw the road signs. Mesas and buttes rose like cathedrals from a dusty red floor, and in the midday sun, they appeared to be bleached white. In the five years since I moved to Denver, I have hiked and camped in the red rock deserts of the Colorado Plateau—along a perennial stream as wildflowers came into bloom, deep in the canyons of the Green River, and in an unexpected winter storm that left snow on our tents and on the budding cotton-woods. Before I came to Denver at twenty-two, I had not stepped foot in the vast landscapes of the American West, though I had seen pictures of the Rockies. This desert, with its endless light and rock, diminutive plant life, and vistas that scorched red to the horizon, had been a revelation. But by the time I came to Monument Valley, a part of this landscape had already seeped into me. The scale of the view no longer jolted me as it once did. It was instead a kind of homecoming.

Monument Valley was something else altogether. After a hundred or so miles of desert at seventy miles per hour, the views began to blend into one another. I thought of Edward Abbey's rant: "A man on foot, on horse-back, or on bicycle will see more, feel more, enjoy more in one mile than the motorized tourists can in a hundred miles." The Colorado Plateau is Abbey's country after all. He may have been cantankerous, and he used the environmental impact of population growth as grounds to argue against immigration, but he loved this desert and wanted us to experience it slowly and fully. As I drove over the last hill, I saw three buttes rise from the wide-open valley, giant sandstone columns atop ruffled skirts of dark mudstone. The word *monument* came to mind and I said aloud, "That has to be Monument Valley." The landscape stood out, but I also had an uneasy sense of déjà vu, as though the image had already been imprinted in my memory.

I knew the valley had been the setting for John Ford's 1939 western *Stagecoach,* the film that gave John Wayne his breakout role as the Ringo Kid. Here's the thing: I grew up in Singapore, fourteen time zones away on the other side of the globe, a crowded island unimaginable in this red rock desert. The western has been exported around the world; as a child, I had watched my share of these films, though between my dissociation at the time and the tropes of the genre, in my mind they collapse into a sea of mountains, deserts, gunfights, and chases. The only film I distinctly remember is Paul Newman and Robert Redford's *Butch Cassidy and the Sundance Kid.* To this day I am still unsure whether I had seen *Stagecoach* in those years. Evidently, my parents did, for it was them who wanted to visit this shrine to Hollywood.

When I got back to Denver, I checked out *Stagecoach* from the library. The film is predictable and yet compelling, as the best of the commercial genres tend to be, reinforcing tropes so deeply embedded in the culture that they appear natural and inevitable. A motley group of strangers—a pregnant young wife on the way to reunite with her cavalry officer husband, an alcoholic doctor and a prostitute both driven out of town, a banker who had embezzled the payroll, a whiskey salesman, and a southern gambler—rides a stagecoach from Tonto, Arizona to Lordsburg, New Mexico. Before they leave Tonto, the cavalry tells them that the Apache warrior Geronimo is on the warpath, but they all have to get to Lordsburg without delay, and the stagecoach leaves. Along the way, they encounter the Ringo Kid, who has broken out of jail and wants to avenge his father and brother, but his horse is injured. The marshal, riding shotgun, recognizes him and takes him into custody. No prizes for guessing what happens next.

The scenes in which the stagecoach runs from one town to another show as the backdrop the Mittens and the Merrick Butte, the three monoliths at the center of Monument Valley, and after a while, I imagined the stagecoach running in circles around this place. In the film, the landscape is stripped of its history and memory—for one, it is located in the Navajo Nation, itself a legacy of settler violence against the Indigenous peoples of the Americas, a story that *Stagecoach* not only elides but turns on its head to portray the Indians as the menacing other—and presented instead as solely an aesthetic phenomenon. It reflects the rugged masculinity of the hero, at once silent and stoic, his strength derived from the voluptuous austerity of the desert, even though John Wayne seemed to me more like an awkward kid than a paragon of manhood.

Like this American desert, the Ringo Kid is located outside of civilized society, without ties to family or culture, loyal only to a higher sense of honor. And in the paradigm of the movie, this is a virtue, the soul of a great man. As expected, he is the only one who treats the prostitute Dallas with dignity, and they quickly fall in love. At a stop before the final stage to Lordsburg, she helps him escape, but when he rides out into the landscape, he sees Apache smoke signals and turns back. The stagecoach leaves despite the warning signs, and a band of Apaches ambushes it. The marshal removes the Kid's handcuffs and hands him a gun, and the Kid rises to the occasion. He rides into Lordsburg in the driver's seat, the ostensible hero of this adventure, but I thought the landscape was the central character of the film.

My parents are not walkers, so they took a drive around the valley, and I went to the Mittens alone. A woman on foot, all that. I wanted to experience the landscape and inhabit the textures of this place, even if fleetingly. On the trail, I came to a dirt road. In the glare, I made out the silhouette of a house. I knew I was on Navajo land and that a few families continue to live here. A few more steps and I was glad to find the trail again; I did not want to trespass into another person's home. Or perhaps, as yet another Hollywood pilgrim, I was already trespassing. The Navajos call this place *Tse'Bii'Ndzisgaii*, of which I have heard a number of translations; a Navajo guide I asked said that its emotional meaning cannot be translated, but it approximates "White Light Shining on Rocks." Unlike the name Monument Valley, it is descriptive rather than prescriptive, concrete instead of abstract, grounded in the senses—in the lived experience—instead of in lofty ideas.

At the far end of West Mitten, far from the shade of the mesa, I looked out into the desert. Cliff roses, Mormon tea, and sagebrush dotted the sand. The air was still. The folds and crevices of the rocks belied the ancient processes of uplift and erosion. I thought of this moment when I later saw the trailer for *Stagecoach* again. The trailer begins with scenes of airplanes and trains in motion. The voiceover says that before this current era of industrialization and acceleration, the stagecoach was the way to travel—a precursor, in a way, to Abbey's rant about industrialized tourists. The visual then cuts to a stagecoach running through Monument Valley. In contrast to the machines, the horses that power the stagecoach represent the primitive forces of nature. The western appeals to this timelessness, this nostalgia for a primordial world.

In 1893, historian Frederick Jackson Turner wrote that the frontier, with its land free for the taking, shaped the American spirit of innovation and democracy. The settlement patterns described in the 1890 US Census indicated that the frontier had disappeared in that most of the usable land had already been claimed by white settlers and thus civilized, so to speak. (The Indigenous peoples who called and still call this land home did not factor into this calculation, other than as savages to be feared and destroyed.) The western was a reaction to this closing of the frontier. It mythologized the ideals of individualism and adventure in the cowboy hero. He is often an outlaw, a man of courage and honor despite, or perhaps precisely because of, his outsider status. When I watched the westerns again, I finally understood the appeal of the Harvard and Yale boy turned brush-clearing Texan cowboy George W. Bush. He wore the mannerisms of an ancient hero.

In westerns, modernity is equated with culture, which is in turn associated with the degradation of the spirit. In *Stagecoach*, only the Ringo Kid treats the prostitute Dallas as an equal, while the others shun her. Culture is conformity and the status quo, while nature represents the individual conscience, authority, and morality, which curiously echoes the ethos of transcendentalists such as Thoreau and Emerson, as well as their spiritual descendant Edward Abbey. Nostalgia is powerful; it erases what is inconvenient for us to see. Ironically, it was in film, a technology that, like trains and airplanes, allowed us to transcend the limits of nature and obliterate the sensory experience, that the western found its apotheosis.

Film combines the narrative drive of story with the visual qualities of photography, which is to say, it allowed us to frame the hero's quest in a magnificent landscape.

There is something to be said about walking, putting one foot before another in the sand, the desert heat on my back, and nothing between my skin and sky. I learned this when I came out West—to slow down and look around me carefully, taking mental notes of the plants that have adapted to this harsh climate, the rocks that change from pink to purple depending on their mineral content, and the quality of light that has drawn painters and photographers alike for more than a hundred years. As much as I take issue with many of Abbey's stances, especially his insular views toward immigration, I also learned how to inhabit a landscape from him. It is a privilege to be able to walk in these wild places, and almost all of us arrive here in some motorized form anyway, but in walking, I learned to name and describe my surroundings. I learned to put words to my experiences. In walking, the most primordial form of locomotion, I taught myself to own what I plainly saw and felt, to access truths I had been raised to find elusive.

At the Mittens, I watched thunderclouds gather in the distance. The celestial drama of shifting clouds and light fascinated me, but I was also trying to time its arrival. The buttes were taller than I was, but the land was open enough that I had nowhere to hide in a lightning storm. I kept walking, imagining myself itinerant in this landscape, the petty concerns of everyday life receding, and nature a bodily encounter without the mediation of a lens. The speed and disembodiment of modern life often feel overwhelming, not to mention the unspoken cruelties with which we put up in the name of civilization. It is easy to find solace in a nostalgic ideal of nature and heroism, to choose not to see beyond the fantasy, to fear that which contradicts our deep-seated beliefs. As much as I sometimes yearned to inhabit a simpler world, I also saw the seduction of this vision, and I knew it had been planted in me long ago.

Coastlines

IN THE FIRST HALF of the twentieth century, a Chinese immigrant carved this poem onto a wall at the Angel Island Immigration Station in the San Francisco Bay. It was unsigned, one of many in the barracks where Chinese immigrants were detained under the exclusion laws of the time:

> The ocean circles a lone peak.
> Rough terrain surrounds this prison.
> There are few birds flying over the cold hills.
> The wild goose messenger cannot find its way.

From 1910 to 1940, Angel Island served as the main port of entry on the West Coast, as Ellis Island did in the New York Harbor. The 1882 Chinese Exclusion Act prohibited people of Chinese descent from entering the United States unless they belonged to one of the exempt classes: merchants, students, teachers, government officials, temporary visitors, US citizens, and their immediate families. The law was intended to keep out unskilled laborers, who were seen as degenerates who took away American jobs, but in practice, the onus was on anyone who looked Chinese to prove their eligibility to land. When boats arrived in San Francisco, most of the Chinese, especially those who claimed to have immediate family in America, were ferried to Angel Island. There, they lived in barracks as they waited for their petitions to be adjudicated.

On Angel Island, inspectors questioned these prospective immigrants and their families about the minutiae of private life, from family trees and village layouts to daily meals and the material of the living room floor. The 1906 San Francisco earthquake destroyed City Hall and many birth and death records held there; in the absence of these documents, officials resorted to testing their knowledge of a shared familial life. If the versions matched, the relationship was deemed valid and the newcomer could land. Discrepancies meant deportation or a long wait on Angel Island for an appeal hearing. Most Chinese stayed on the island for two or three weeks if their cases were straightforward, but some were detained for months and even years as they waited for their appeals.

In this limbo, some detainees wrote poems on the barrack walls. Many scribbled on the walls in ink, but some of them also carved their words into the wood. They treated the horizontal wooden panels like lines in a notebook, modeling their verses after classical Chinese poetry, writing vertically from right to left. Where one poem ends the next begins. Most of these poems are unsigned, likely to avoid retribution from the guards, but some of the poets inscribed their surnames and hometowns. Most of the detainees were young men who had borrowed money or depleted their families' savings for their journeys to America, hoping to strike it rich, send money home, and eventually reunite with their kin. Failing their interrogations meant failing their families, and some committed suicide instead of returning to China in shame. They wrote about homesickness, broken dreams, anxious futures, and fears of disappointing the family. In these poems, the cold fog of the San Francisco Bay heightened the isolation of this prison. Some vowed to exact revenge on the barbaric Americans. Some affirmed a determination to succeed in spite of the obstacles in their way. Some compared their plight to Napoleon's exile on Saint Helena.

*

The day before I came to Angel Island, I hiked the coast of Point Reyes with some friends. Point Reyes is a cape just north of San Francisco, jutting into the sea like a hook. The lighthouse at its westernmost point used to warn ships sailing from the San Francisco Bay of their proximities to the coast. Sometimes the fog was so thick that the sailors could not see the flashing lights, and on these days, the lighthouse would sound a foghorn. But ships would still wreck on the rocky coast and the lighthouse sent lookout men to walk the beaches. They could not send final warnings, but they could respond to crews who found themselves in the cold Pacific waters.

At Point Reyes, we looked out at the sea, pale on a cloudy day. We walked on cliffs that overlooked the water and up grassy hills full of stinging nettles and poison oak. On the ridge, we came to a forest of Douglas fir, the trees dark giants trapping the fog. The fog dripped like very light rain and turned the trail into a mud war. The mud rose and fell with each footstep and soaked our shoes. I wondered why all four guys tiptoed at the edge of the trail, and they wondered why I walked through the mud, until one of them pointed out that I had waterproof boots. Another guy grabbed a handful of stinging nettles while trying to get around the mud. When we walked out of the forest, the ground was dry again. In a distant valley, the fog parted to reveal hills golden in the middle of summer.

A coast is where land meets water; it is a natural border. Here tides rise and inundate beaches or recede to reveal sandbars. Waves erode headlands and reshape bays and beaches. The law may differentiate an immigrant from a citizen, but like the coast, laws can change. Our beliefs can change, with our sense of justice or irrational fears. At Point Reyes, the coast changed with each footstep we planted on the ground, muddy or otherwise. In the span of our long hike, we passed sandy cliffs, lush carpets of poison oak, dark forests, dusty green shrubs, and golden hills. The sea appeared as a vision of the infinite, our gazes taken to the fog in the sky.

*

The day after I went to Angel Island, I walked from Fisherman's Wharf to the Golden Gate Bridge alone. The coast where I found bliss is also a military fort. Fort Mason was built during the Civil War to defend the city against the Confederacy, though it was unlikely that a gun was fired from here, given the nautical distance from the South. The Army continued to use it as a staging and discharge area for troops in the Spanish-American War, the Indian campaigns, and World War I. It was expanded during World War II to serve the Pacific theater. Next to Fort Mason is Marina Green, a wealthy enclave complete with yacht clubs, built on landfill from the 1906 earthquake. The land liquefied in the 1989 Loma Prieta earthquake and the buildings collapsed, but the rich rebuilt for the views of the sea.

Down the coast is Crissy Field, an old airfield and the landing strip for early transcontinental flights. In the late 1800s, the railroads shrank the continent from months in wagons to weeks in cabins. These flights covered New York to San Francisco in days. In 1920, the first such flight landed at Crissy Field after thirty-four hours in the air and seventy-five hours after its departure from New York. Four years later, the first dawn to dusk transcontinental flight landed at Crissy Field and collapsed continental travel into a day. Crissy Field closed in 1974, the military bases in the 1990s, and the land is now restored as tidal wetlands and sand dunes. At an estuary, I saw seabirds walking on the marshes. Dune grasses crept onto the sand. Shrubs bloomed dots of pink and lavender. Beyond the bridge, I glimpsed the sea again.

*

The Angel Island coast ruffles into headlands and coves like skirts. It was a national border, and like most borders, it remained porous. As the 1906 earthquake destroyed many records, Chinese men living in the United States could claim unrelated persons as family. A system of paper sons emerged in the Chinese community. For a fee, a man would sponsor unrelated men as his sons. Brokers drew up coaching papers, small booklets of fictitious family histories to tell the immigration officers at Angel Island. The paper sons memorized these details during the voyage and tossed the papers into the sea before they arrived in the San Francisco Bay. The officers knew the ruse; one of them remarked that if all these stories were true, then each Chinese woman living in America before 1900 would have had 500 children. But they had to prove familial ties without reliable documents, matching recollections of the trivialities of family life instead, the facts they thought they could prove instead of the fluid terrains of blood and emotions. Ironically, the paper sons who had to invent their families learned the stories well and were more likely to pass the interrogations.

The real sons, more secure in their sense of family, sometimes faltered, especially if the rice bin had been moved after the father left home.

How do we regard truth and credibility in the face of a broken and unjust system?

*

The Chinese language was the bane of my school years. In Singapore, where I grew up, each student is required to learn their mother tongue as their second language. This policy is meant to inculcate us in our cultures and traditions, which is noble in spirit and a departure from actual practice. In the classroom, instead of discussing literature or engaging in spirited debates, we learned the language as a collection of phrases to be memorized. We treated it as a static body of knowledge, like the compounds of organic chemistry, rather than as a form of speech and a means of conveying ideas, meaning, and emotions. Though I spoke some Chinese at home, the language has always felt abstract to me, an isolated academic subject rather than a part of my identity.

As a child, I also heard in the words *tradition* and *heritage* a plot to keep me in my place, dutiful and compliant. Unlike the selfish and hedonistic West, we who were steeped in our Chinese traditions were purportedly decent people who respected authority. In particular, we were to keep our bodies under control, straitjacketed into the trappings of propriety. The body, I now know, is the source of speech, and speech is the foundation of language. "Censor the body and you censor breath and speech at the same time," Hélène Cixous wrote. In these words, I saw the condition of my childhood—unable to speak. I inhabited instead the stories others designed for me. Fairly or not, I associated Chinese culture with this silence, and when I came to America at nineteen, I was glad to be freed of the language.

*

The morning I came to Angel Island, fog hung low on the bay. I watched waves roll up on the sliver of beach near the barracks and spread across the sand like knuckles. I came with a friend who grew up in Beijing and was about to be sworn in as a US citizen. Though Angel Island lies in neither of our personal histories, as immigrants and women of Chinese descent, we wanted to see the place and the poems for ourselves. After decades of exposure and neglect, most of the poems had already faded into the wood. They would have vanished altogether had a park ranger not spotted them before the buildings were slated for demolition.

We visited a room in the men's barracks that had been converted into a museum. The crevices on the walls occasionally yielded the shape of a Chinese character, a word or two still legible from the poems. Most of the words looked familiar to me, but I could not pronounce them. As I walked along the peeling walls, I noticed two poems still legible in their entirety. I looked at the inscriptions with a mix of terror and familiarity; I had an inkling of what they said, even though I could barely read the words. I also recognized the way I tend to dissociate around the Chinese language. Most strangely, I felt the rhythms, intonations, and lyricism of the poems, reverberations that began deep in my body.

My friend read a poem aloud to me in Mandarin, the dialect of the capital in the north and the official language that we learned in school. As she enunciated each word, I began to recognize the images and meanings, the wind and night and fog, in the poem. I felt the loneliness of the landscape and the anxiety of detention, but I could not process the emotions. I pressed a button on the signboard below the poems and a disembodied voice recited it in Cantonese, the dialect of the southern province from which most of the immigrants came. Cantonese I do not know at all—my family is Hokkien, from the next province—and in this dialect, the words sounded strange to my ears and the images became abstract again.

The signboard also had an English translation of the poem. The two languages have different sentence structures and modes of making meaning. In this translation, much of the form, rhythm, and lyric compression are lost, but I could finally read the poem, which begins:

In the quiet of the night, I heard, faintly, the whistling of wind.
The forms and shadows saddened me; upon seeing the landscape, I composed a poem.
The floating clouds, the fog, darken the sky.

*

In the 1930s, detainees Jann Mon Fong and Tet Yee copied down many poems and snuck the manuscripts into San Francisco when they landed. In the 1970s, when California State Parks ranger Alexander Weiss stumbled upon these wall writings in a derelict building, he told San Francisco State College professor George Araki about his find. Araki, whose Japanese mother had spent time on Angel Island, brought photographer Mak Takahashi to document the inscriptions. In 1980, Him Mark Lai, Judy Yung, and Genny Lim, all of whose parents had been detained on Angel Island, compiled the poems from these three sources, together with translations and oral histories, into an anthology titled *Island: Poetry and History of Chinese Immigrants on Angel Island*. The translations I have quoted here are from this book. The authors also write that they found it hard to get former detainees, including their own parents, to talk about their experiences. Some had a lingering fear of retribution, but many did not want to relive the shame and humiliation of their imprisonment. They would rather have kept silent, even and especially with their children.

Unlike the fading words on the walls, this book seeks to preserve and interpret the poems. It renders them in their cultural and historical context even as it removes them from their setting, their psychogeography. I first read *Island* at home in Denver, seven years into my life in America. At that time, I was on a work visa I had obtained through a lottery process. The year I applied, there were three times more applications than available visas, and in the absence of political will to change the quota, the US Citizenship and Immigration Services held a lottery to determine which petitions they would review. I won the lottery, but I also knew that my future was shaped by such arbitrary winds. In Denver, I had begun to write. I was drawn to the landscapes of the American West and the ways these places shape our perspectives, and in the Angel Island poems, I saw a crucible of the questions I had been asking about landscape, language, and borders.

In imperial China, it was a crime to write unofficial histories. Travelers inscribed subversive thoughts on poetry boards anonymously at rest stops, inns, and even on trees and snow. At Angel Island, I saw that the detainees had used the barrack walls as a kind of poetry board, a space in which they could chronicle their journeys to America and give voice to a history that would not otherwise be told. They could express the pain they might not speak about again for the rest of their lives. As I looked at the poems on the walls, I wished I knew the Chinese language better. Despite this linguistic border, I saw in these verses an indomitable spirit in the face of suffering. In writing poetry, these detainees spoke in the face of silence, inscribing truths deeper than the "facts" they had to perform for the immigration inspectors, drawing out a language rooted in bodies that cannot cross the San Francisco Bay.

*

At Point Reyes, we reached Alamere Falls, a waterfall that plunged off the crumbling cliffs into the Pacific. Two of the guys had walked ahead, and when I caught up with them, they were standing on the dry bed of the falls, saying, "I thought with all the water we had on the ridge, we would see a huge waterfall!" Alamere Creek had shriveled to its narrowest channel, and the water flickered down the cliff. We climbed down a sandy bluff to the beach. I waded into the sea, my feet still dry in my boots, as Alamere Falls pooled behind me, feeding the ever-shifting coast.

Dreams of Golden Mountain

AT MANHATTAN'S BATTERY PARK, I watched waves roil on the concrete banks. In the distance, I saw Ellis Island, the great immigration portal through which millions of people from Europe came between 1892 and 1954. Across the grey waters of the New York Harbor, the Statue of Liberty raised her torch to the sky. Inscribed on a plaque is Emma Lazarus's sonnet "The New Colossus," with these famous last lines:

> Give me your tired, your poor,
> Your huddled masses yearning to breathe free,
> The wretched refuse of your teeming shore.
> Send these, the homeless, tempest-tost to me,
> I lift my hand beside the golden door.

I thought of Angel Island in the San Francisco Bay, where thousands of Chinese immigrants were detained under the Chinese Exclusion Act. Some of them wrote poems on the barrack walls, including this one:

> The insects chirp outside the four walls.
> The inmates often sigh.
> Thinking of affairs back home,
> Unconscious tears wet my lapel.

Ellis Island had its problems, and there were narrow quotas for immigrants from southern and eastern Europe. But for the most part, Ellis Island was more about inclusion than exclusion, acceptance than refusal. Angel Island, on the other hand, was designed to keep out the Chinese. America has not been the land of the free for everyone.

The first Chinese came to America during the 1849 California gold rush. Like many who arrived on the West Coast from around the world, they dreamed of striking it rich; they referred to California, the Sierra, and later much of the American West as *gam saan,* or Golden Mountain. They worked in the mines, turned the deserts of the San Joaquin Valley into arable farmland, and built the transcontinental railroads. Most of them came from the Canton province in southern China, which had been impoverished by the Opium War and the rebellions against the Manchurian Qing Dynasty. They hoped to make their fortunes and return to their families in China.

In America, they lived in their own enclaves, or Chinatowns, where they had their own grocers, laundries, and opium dens. Many of the laboring class spoke little to no English and could not read or write. The whites saw the Chinese, with their different language and customs and their insular communities, as unwilling or unable to assimilate. They treated the Chinese with animosity, often relegating them to the most backbreaking and least profitable jobs. Between 1852 and 1878, the California legislature passed a raft of legislation aimed at the Chinese, including a tax on non-citizens working in the mines, the exclusion of Chinese children from public schools, and a ban on Chinese owning real estate.

In September 1873, Philadelphia brokerage house Jay Cook & Company filed for bankruptcy and precipitated a bank panic. It had overextended itself speculating on railroads, and when it could not raise enough capital to meet its liabilities, investors began a run on the bank. The stock market cratered so badly that the New York Stock Exchange closed for ten days. Across the country, banks and railroads failed. On top of that, the 1869 completion of the first transcontinental railroad, the Union Pacific-Central Pacific from Omaha to Sacramento, put many people, white and Chinese alike, out of work.

White demagogues blamed Chinese laborers for their woes. They accused the Chinese of being willing to work at lower wages and break strikes. Racial riots broke out in Los Angeles, San Francisco, Denver, and Rock Springs, Wyoming, among other places across the West. In July 1877, a labor rally outside San Francisco's City Hall devolved into a riot in Chinatown that lasted two days, the violence quelled only when the police and state militia intervened. The following month, Irish labor leader and provocateur Denis Kearney founded the Workingman's Trade and Labor Union of San Francisco, adopting the slogan, "The Chinese Must Go!" He stated his priorities as thus: "When the Chinese question is settled, we can discuss whether it would be better to hang, shoot, or cut the capitalists into pieces."

In 1882, Congress passed the Chinese Exclusion Act and President Chester Arthur signed it into law. It marked the first time America sought to close rather than open its borders. It was also one of the first US laws that restricted immigration based on race.

This is the milieu in which Wong Chin Foo came to America. The subject of Scott D. Seligman's biography *The First Chinese American: The Remarkable Life of Wong Chin Foo,* Wong was a writer, public speaker, and activist in the late nineteenth century who fought the Chinese Exclusion Act. He was not the first Chinese person in America, nor was he the first to be naturalized, but he was among the first to adopt western dress and write in English for a white audience. He was also, according to Seligman, the first to use the term *Chinese American;* it was the English translation of the name of his first Chinese language newspaper.

Wong was unlike the Cantonese laborers who made up most of the Chinese in America. In fact, he looked down on his southern brethren, a prejudice that would mark his later efforts to fight for Chinese enfranchisement. Born in northern China to a wealthy family that lost its fortune, he and his father were taken in by a Southern Baptist missionary, Sallie Holmes. In 1868, Holmes brought him to America to complete his education, hoping that he would become a missionary and preach Christianity to the Chinese. Instead, he cut classes to go on the lecture circuit, speaking about Chinese culture to an East Coast audience, who, unlike their counterparts in the West, had little contact with people of his race.

His flair for theatrics made him popular with the whites. He returned to China in 1870 without completing school.

In 1873, after a failed attempt to overthrow the Qing Dynasty, Wong returned to America, leaving behind a wife and a newborn son. When his boat arrived in San Francisco, he tipped off the authorities to a prostitution ring on the vessel, earning him the enmity of the gangs that ruled the city's Chinatown. He survived an attempt on his life and fled eastward. Unlike the America of his student days, where hostilities toward the Chinese remained mostly in the West, the country as a whole was moving toward Chinese exclusion. In 1874, he successfully applied for US citizenship in Grand Rapids, Michigan. For most of his life in America, he lived in Chicago and New York, writing and lecturing on Chinese customs, food, and history for white audiences. His work appeared in the major newspapers of the time, including the *New York Times, Washington Post,* and *Boston Globe.*

Wong also struggled with what it meant to be Chinese in America. The whites who sought Chinese exclusion painted them as dishonest and depraved heathens who worshiped idols and ate rats and dogs. In response, Wong argued that the basic ideals of Chinese culture were similar to those of Western civilization, just manifested in different ways. He offered five hundred dollars to anyone who could show him a Chinese person who ate a rat. In a stunt, he also styled himself as the first Confucian missionary to America. At first, he did not try to refute or attack Christianity, taking aim instead at the missionaries. The missionaries may have taken him in as a child and given him an education, but it is likely he resented their condescension toward the Chinese, whom they saw as lost souls waiting to be saved. In any case, he criticized their methods as patronizing and ineffective.

In 1887, five years after the passage of the Chinese Exclusion Act, he published the essay "Why Am I a Heathen" in the *North American Review.* It marked his break with Christianity, pitted American norms against those of the Chinese, and became his most well-known and controversial piece. He condemned Christianity and its hypocrisies. He made fun of sectarian arguments among the Christian denominations and said that in studying them, he did not arrive at any spiritual revelations. Heathenism, which he equated with Chinese culture, led to a more just society, though his characterization of China as a nation of harmonious families without strife or dishonesty seemed more a product of a fervid and perhaps nostalgic imagination. And in his typical hyperbolic, bombastic way, he asserted that the Christian tradition derived from the older and superior Chinese civilization.

In the preface to *The First Chinese American,* Seligman writes that he first came across Wong in a list of prominent Chinese Americans. One of the few from the nineteenth century, Wong was described as an early civil rights activist who opposed the Chinese Exclusion Act. Seligman writes,

> Since I had believed that few Chinese Americans had risen to national prominence during the nineteenth century and that the community more or less cowered in a defensive crouch, permitting the hated legislation to be brought down on their heads without much protest, I resolved to try to learn a bit more about this Mr. Wong and his accomplishments.

That is to say, in writing this biography, Seligman seeks to bring Wong's life and achievements into the light and dispel the stereotype of the Chinese as meek and subservient.

And Wong's life and work make for a colorful biography. He did not see his wife and son for twenty-five years, nor was it likely that he sent money to support them. As a US citizen, he could have sponsored his family to come to America, though, to be fair, the 1875 Page Act denied admission to suspected Chinese prostitutes, which in effect meant that all Chinese immigrant women had to prove their virtue at the US consulate in Hong Kong and again at their port of entry, usually San Francisco, a humiliation most respectable women did not want to undergo. He started many ventures but seldom had the will to see them through. He was often reckless and impulsive; it was unlikely he could have supported a family. And he could not return to China even for brief visits: he would lose his US citizenship, and he believed that he was still wanted by Qing officials.

Wong was often drawn to conflict, sometimes out of a higher purpose and sometimes, it seems, to enhance his own notoriety. He riled up powerful Chinatown families, especially in his crusade to eradicate the vices of prostitution and opium in the community. Unlike most Chinese, who kept their grievances within the confines of Chinatown, he often turned to American courts for redress. He challenged Denis Kearney to a debate, and when the Irishman turned him down, he insinuated that he must be illiterate, a charge often lobbed at the Chinese to justify their exclusion, and proposed a duel instead, giving the demagogue his choice of weapon, "chopsticks, Irish potatoes, or Krupp guns," and pledged to pay half his bail.

Wong opposed the Chinese Exclusion Act, writing that most Chinese wanted only to work hard and return to China, and those who chose to stay would assimilate into American society. He reminded Americans of the promise of the Statue of Liberty, "Is this not the country that boasted of its free and liberal institutions—the land of the oppressed and the home of the unfortunate?" In 1881, when the passage of the exclusion law—which included a ban on all Chinese from gaining US citizenship—was apparent, he brought three Chinese to the courts to petition for naturalization, a stunt meant to garner attention and test the system. And when the law passed, he founded his own newspaper, the *Chinese American*. In a climate where most Chinese in America could not read English, he intended it as a way for his compatriots to follow national developments.

He also pressed his fellow Chinese to become more involved in politics. In 1892, when Congress debated the Geary Act, which would extend and strengthen the Chinese Exclusion Act, he organized the Chinese Equal Rights League to lobby for Chinese enfranchisement and even testified before Congress on the matter. By then, his views toward the Chinese Exclusion Act had changed. He became favorable to the ban on new immigrants, contending they were lowly Cantonese laborers who were unable to acculturate, a stance that echoed the rhetoric of the demagogues. Instead, he sought only the repeal of the naturalization clause. In his view, US citizenship was a right only for Americanized Chinese like himself, who adopted western ways and appearances, spoke and wrote English, and saw their futures in America.

As a biographer, Seligman is informative and entertaining. He quotes articles by and about Wong liberally, often to great comic effect. He does not shrink from Wong's contradictions even as he champions his achievements. He shows us the Wong who wrote that educated Chinese should have equal rights to slaves from the African jungle. He insists that Wong, as one of the first Chinese in America who publicly wrestled with his identity, at home neither among the Chinese nor the whites, defined a path for generations of Chinese Americans to come. And in writing Wong's story, he also draws a portrait of American society during the Chinese exclusion era and by implication, questions America's self-belief as the land of the free.

But as much as Wong's story is an important part of American history, Seligman's tack does not do it the justice that it deserves. The Chinese Exclusion Act may have been repealed in 1943 with the Magnuson Act, but the underlying prejudices have not changed. They have merely shifted in form, and while anti-Chinese bigotry persists, nowadays the immigrant bogeyman is for the most part another race, but Seligman does not elucidate or question them. In his obsession with what made Wong the first Chinese American and the cultural divide that Wong had to straddle, he misses an important thread: What does it mean that Wong, in his efforts to assimilate, had to struggle with his faith? And more importantly, what does it mean that Wong eventually abandoned the fight against the ban on new immigrants and focused on the path to citizenship for educated and assimilated Chinese instead?

There is nothing wrong with assimilation in itself, but it should not be a basis for granting civil rights. Yet Seligman is more interested in analyzing whether Wong is more or less Chinese based on his degree of assimilation, a game of cultural identity based on superficial differences, which carries the implication that racial difference is a valid ground for discrimination. On this same note, Seligman does not look at how Wong fell into the xenophobic trap of considering some immigrants "good" and others "bad" and privileging the former at the expense of the latter. He is content with telling this denouement to Wong's story as it is, as if Wong's eventual identification with the prejudices of power was inevitable, an integral part of becoming American.

It is not sufficient to hold up an exceptional person from a targeted group as an exemplar to address the injustices against the group. Seligman fails to consider the implicit question when we talk about human rights: whom do we include and whom do we exclude? Who do we consider 'us,' worthy of our acceptance and empathy, and 'them,' undeserving of our concern?

Firecracker

I HEARD THE PERCUSSION FIRST, the *dong-chiang, dong-dong-chiang* of the drums and cymbals that accompanied the lion dance. The rhythms shook in my body and drowned out the traffic around the Far East Center in west Denver. The crowd on this first day of Chinese New Year spanned multigenerational Chinese families, curious onlookers from the suburbs and the adjacent Hispanic enclave, white couples with adopted Chinese daughters, mixed-race couples and their children, and recent immigrants like my partner and me. We walked toward the stage on which the lions danced and looked for my Aunt Deborah.

The lions were each red, blue, yellow, or black, with furry white trimmings like fish scales. Two men propped up each costume, one at the head and the other at the tail, their faces hidden by the bright cloth. Two lions leaped onto the support beam that served as a makeshift stage as the others looked on. They battled each other, ate red packets, and even paused to rest and sleep. The highly stylized movements resembled the martial arts. Shop owners hired the troupes to perform in front of their premises, a gesture they believed would bring luck and prosperity in the coming year. In doing so, they also created a street party in the midwinter chill.

In the traditional southern-style lion dance, the lion embodies Nian, a mythological beast that descends on villages around the new year, destroying crops, attacking children, and otherwise wreaking havoc.

In one such attack, the villagers scared the beast away by lavishly display-
ing the color red, banging their pots and pans, and setting off firecrackers.
Afterward, they decided to preempt the beast every year by dancing in the
streets, flaunting the color red, and making a lot of noise. The lion dance
emerged from this symbolic slaying of the beast. It has since evolved into
a celebration, the lions turned into emblems and life, luck, and happiness,
but the rousing percussion and the color red remain.

I left Singapore for America at nineteen, and I have rarely celebrated
Chinese New Year since. For most of my childhood, I associated the
holiday with putting up appearances, constructing a false self to placate
the family, and playing a role that conforms to other people's expecta-
tions. In the early years of my adulthood, I knew, even if I could not
articulate it, that I had to strip away the masks and recover the self I had
to hide. I did not miss Chinese New Year. But this year, Aunt Deborah,
my mother's cousin who, as it happened, also lives in Denver, invited us
to join her, her son, and her partner for the lion dance at the Far East
Center, after which we would adjourn for dim sum. "One of the houses
between your mum's and ours had a troupe every year," she had told me.
"I grew up waking to the firecrackers and drums, and Chinese New Year
isn't the same without it."

The day before Chinese New Year, I happened to read Rebecca Solnit's essay "We Won't Bow Down," in which she describes the civil society
and sense of community that arises from the largest public celebration
in America, the weeks-long Carnival in New Orleans that culminates in
Mardi Gras. Carnival begins on Twelfth Night and ends on the day before
Lent, and Mardi Gras is known for its big parades and riotous parties.
Carnival, Solnit argues,

> reinforces joy and ownership of public space and a kind of confi-
> dence in coexisting with a wide array of strangers. New Orleans
> itself is the place where, unlike the rest of the United States, slaves
> were not so cut off from the chances to gather and chances to
> maintain their traditions . . . They didn't bow down. This is some-
> thing to celebrate, and it is what is celebrated by some people in
> the streets.

The traditional Chinese New Year rites begin on the eve with a family reunion dinner. The first day is usually spent visiting paternal relatives and the second day visiting maternal relatives. The rest of the fifteen days are spent alternating among rest, gathering and feasting with family and friends, making offerings to the ancestors and gods, and on the last day, attending a street festival. But this is when you have fifteen days off from work and school, which, in this modern capitalist age, rarely happens anymore. The celebrations I knew in Singapore were truncated to the second day, which is to say, Chinese New Year became a retreat from the streets. And firecrackers have been restricted since 1970 and outright banned in 1972, after a massive accident that caused multiple injuries and fatalities.

Admittedly, my family did not attend Chingay, the Singapore street festival staged around the fifteenth day. We favored the apparent order of the home over the clamor of the streets; I grew up with a sense of self that was isolated and alienated in private life. Because we were part of Singapore's cultural majority, our ways are taken to be the norm, the core of the social landscape. We did not need to assert our ownership of public space. We did not need to make our presence known. And in a culture of cutthroat competition, public life is seen as wasteful, a squandering of precious time that could be better put toward getting ahead. But Chingay also strikes me as officious, organized from the top rather than from the ground, turning us into passive spectators rather than creators with agency. And the street festival was adopted only after the government had outlawed firecrackers; Chingay was the official substitute for the spirit of Chinese New Year.

Chinese New Year in Denver is a far cry from Carnival, but it is a public celebration in a city where the historic Chinatown is no longer there and is remembered, if at all, for the race riot in 1880. (Two years before the passage of the Chinese Exclusion Act, two white men and two Chinese men got into an altercation at a pool hall on Wazee Street, and it escalated into a city-wide riot in which one Chinese man was lynched.) The largest public procession in Denver may be the annual National Western Stock Show parade in January, in which cowboys, cowgirls, and Texas longhorns march down Seventeenth Street amid the skyscrapers of the financial district. The Stock Show does not have as big an impact on Denver's culture and economy as Carnival has on New Orleans's, but it is a break in routine and brings people to the streets. Chinese New Year has an even smaller impact on Denver, but when I went to the Far East Center, I saw it as a primer for street celebrations.

"It's usually a zoo," Aunt Deborah had said. Later, she would tell us that this year's turnout was smaller than usual, likely because of the cold spell. It had snowed the night before and snow still lined the streets; usually, it would melt in a day. Despite the cold, we, Chinese and non-Chinese alike, had gathered at the Far East Center to enjoy the rhythms of the lion dance. I watched a children's troupe set up lions and a dragon in front of a Vietnamese restaurant. The children would have had a feast with their families the night before, and now they were going to perform in public. I don't know how much they did it out of their own volition and how much to appease their parents, but I saw that consciously or not, they were negotiating a space for themselves as individuals and for the Chinese community in Denver's social fabric.

The *shifu* beat the drums. The children clashed the cymbals. A dozen children picked up the sticks and propped up the dragon. The long orange cloth billowed in the wind, a lithe body flowing behind the dragonhead. The moves of the dragon dance are similar to those of the lion dance, both taken from the martial arts, but in the dragon dance, the cloth does not cover the faces of the dancers. Another group of children pulled tiny lion costumes over their heads and fanned out into the crowd, wriggling the beaded eyes and kicking up the tails, feeding on red packets stuffed with a token sum or chocolates wrapped in gold foil.

A dancer lit the firecrackers. The red rolls crackled and the chains burst, filling the air with smoke. The volume of the explosions enveloped even the drums and cymbals and reverberated in my bones. I stood there in a state between shock and euphoria, between a desire to dissolve into the sound and a desire to recoil from the fragments of paper and gunpowder flying everywhere. It was the first time I had experienced live firecrackers, and the only thing I have seen that matched its force is an avalanche in the high peaks west of Denver, where I watched a slab of wet snow crumble on a rocky ledge, shaking the ground and echoing in the valley like thunder. I could see the danger of firecrackers, especially if they are used carelessly, but in this barrage of sound, I also sensed a slipping of the self. My skin seemed permeable, though I knew it was only an illusion.

At the Ruins

MESA VERDE, COLORADO—The cities of stone are set into alcoves in the cliffs, ruins after centuries of abandonment. The walls are cemented with bricks chiseled from the sandstone. They rise a floor or two to a broken ceiling; they sink into the earth; their doorways open into dark chambers. Mesa Verde, *green table,* lies between the southern Rockies and the red rock desert beyond. It was named by the Spanish who sought a route from Santa Fe to the Pacific; to them, the sparse woodlands must have seemed lush after the desert scrub. Deep canyons cross the plateau, ancient rivers scoured the sandstone into cliffs and skirts, and wind and water eroded alcoves into the cliffs. A thousand years ago, people built these cities, accessible only by precarious hand and toe holds on the cliffs. They left in the late thirteenth century. Left to the elements, the cities disintegrated. The walls crumbled. The sandstone calved boulders and crushed the walls. Seven centuries later, the ruins stand as a testament to the mystique of absence.

In the late nineteenth century, American ranchers stumbled on these ruins while on the cattle trail and thought that the people who had built them had vanished. They asked the local Navajo about who had lived here, and the Navajo said the Anasazi, and for decades, the word *Anasazi* came to mean the lost ones. No one knew where they went, or so the story went, a story that fit into the European narrative of America as an

uninhabited continent that awaited their arrival. The cliff dwellings of
Mesa Verde and similar ruins in this area are evidence of civilizations
before Columbus. Their descendants, it turned out, are still around, living with the Pueblo Indians in New Mexico's Rio Grande Valley. In the
former story, time is discrete and history an isolated sequence of events;
in the latter, time and landscape are joined by migrations and memories
passed down over generations.

The people have gone elsewhere. The buildings are still here, in vary-
ing states of ruin. "Decay is the negative image of history," wrote the
landscape historian J. B. Jackson. Decay: to decline, disintegrate. History: the passage of time. Negative image: the inversion of a normal
image, in which light appears as dark and dark as light. These ruins are
the marks of time on the landscape. The desert helped preserve these
ruins. The walls outline cities, across which the shadows of the past flicker.
The ruins that the ranchers, archaeologists, and pothunters found were
not the orderly and empty rooms we see nowadays but mounds of rubble,
turquoise, seashells, dried corn husks, broken pottery, and human bones,
all under layers of rock and sand. The artifacts are now in museums and
on the black market. Archaeologists have stabilized the remains, and in
some places, they have reconstructed the missing parts.

From the mesa top, we walked down steep steps and narrow passageways to Cliff Palace. We crouched on a ledge with a dozen or so other
people and looked across a canyon of spruces and junipers to the jumble
of walls as the ranger told us that Cliff Palace had a hundred and fifty
rooms and twenty-three kivas, those subterranean ceremonial chambers.
Cliff Palace was likely used for gatherings and ceremonies rather than res-
idence, the center of community life at Mesa Verde. The people collected
water from seep springs at the back of the alcove and when the water
started to dry up, they used their urine to make the mortar instead. I had
earlier seen the pit and mud houses on the mesa top. The cliff dwellings,
I saw, were the apotheosis of this civilization, where their masonry and
knowledge of the land came together to create a grand architecture.

Cliff Palace had been a work in progress. New rooms were con-
structed and old ones renovated as the people modified the place to
suit their needs. It was occupied for at most a hundred years. Droughts
plagued the region at the turn of the fourteenth century. Life, already

at the margins, became impossible. The crops failed. The people left, some west to Arizona, some south to New Mexico. The stories of the modern Pueblo people encompass Mesa Verde, but given the history of white-Indigenous relations, the Puebloans are understandably unwilling to divulge them. A story is not just a recital of facts. A story interprets the world and reflects who we are. A story is not fixed in time and space but carried across the landscape as memory. Stories decay with each telling, a detail lost here, another interpretation made there. And in the absence of knowledge, we turn to conjecture. How did they leave? Did they return to pick up something left behind? Has anyone else since lived here?

A city rose and fell. After the fall, it lay open to the wind and water and sun, the walls no longer replastered, the timber beams no longer replaced. Other people may have lived here since, but the record is uncertain. The site upon which the ranchers stumbled was one of abandonment, the buildings no longer in use, the stories in crumbles. Abandon is the story we tell even as we come to occupy the place, building roads and lodges and campgrounds for those of us who venture into this far corner of southwestern Colorado, clearing the rooms of their artifacts. And we seem to think of Mesa Verde in terms of ancient history and distant times. Ruins speak of rise and fall, but at Mesa Verde, I saw the present. Maybe it was the way the noonday light glared in the summer sky and the intense heat turned the body reptilian. As the body slows, so does our sense of time. This light embalmed the ruins; it rained from the sky and bleached the sandstone; it reached into the canyons and promised the beyond.

II
Ordinary Legacies

Western Journeys

THE GREAT AMERICAN DESERT

The West, wrote Bernard DeVoto, begins where the average annual precipitation drops below twenty inches, the level at which irrigation becomes necessary to sustain agriculture. By this definition, the West begins around the hundredth longitudinal meridian, which cuts from North Dakota to Texas and is often seen as the border between the arid and the arable, the wild and the civilized. In the first decade of the nineteenth century, soldier and explorer Zebulon Pike wrote of the grasslands and steppes that collide with the Rocky Mountains, "These vast plains of the western hemisphere may become in time equally celebrated as the sandy deserts of Africa." In the 1820s, surveyor Stephen Long described these high plains as the Great American Desert, devoid of trees and "wholly unfit for cultivation and of course uninhabitable by a people depending on agriculture."

By the 1860s, the United States was rapidly expanding west. Men, women, and children piled into wagons and headed to California and Colorado and places in between with dreams of striking gold. In 1862, Abraham Lincoln signed the Homestead Act, under which any person in good standing with the federal government could obtain a freehold title of up to 160 acres of undeveloped land outside of the original thirteen colonies. The Act harkened the yeoman farmer idealized by Thomas Jefferson, and it gave each man, including freed slaves, a patch of land on which he could raise his family through pious toil. It did not, however, account for the sharp decline in arability west of the hundredth meridian, nor did it provide for government loans or grants for the journey, the construction of homes, and the purchase of farm equipment and seed.

In an 1878 report, geologist and surveyor John Wesley Powell concluded that 160 acres were too broad a brush for the arid West, too much for one man to irrigate but too little to support a family without irrigation. And not all western land could be equally put to use. The alpine tundra is blasted by wind and snow, rock faces are useless as crop and rangelands, and some places are just too far from reliable water sources. He proposed that instead of arbitrarily dividing the land on a rectangular grid, the shape of each homestead should be determined by topography, and each should contain a good water supply. He also suggested a system of cooperation among homesteaders in the same watershed. Congress ignored his recommendations. The 1870s ushered in a wet cycle; as the plains were settled, it seemed, the streams rose. Many pioneers believed that God blessed them with rain for their pious toil. The plow, said Charles Dana Wilbur, "is the instrument which separates civilization from savagery, and converts a desert into a farm or garden . . . To be more concise, *rain follows the plow*."

Dust storms followed the plow instead. A drought arrived in the late 1880s and lingered for a decade. Farms failed. Many homesteaders had borrowed for their journey and equipment, and they defaulted on their loans. The banks repossessed the lands and consolidated their holdings across the plains. A more extensive drought came in the years of the Great Depression. The overgrazed and over-farmed soil turned to dust and darkened the sky all the way to New York. Many more lost their homes and farms, and they packed up for California.

ARRIVALS AND DEPARTURES

In September 1873, three years before Colorado became a state, English traveler Isabella Bird boarded the transcontinental railroad at Truckee,

California, and alighted a week later in Cheyenne, Wyoming. She was on her way back to England from the Sandwich Islands, as the Hawaiian Islands were then known, and had planned a detour to the Rockies. There was already a railroad from Cheyenne to Denver, but she chose to ride horseback across the plains and spent a month in the mountain splendor of Estes Park. In October, she came down to Denver to change horses, meet with the territorial governor, and plan her route through South Park, and of the ride she wrote,

> It is a dreary ride of thirty miles over the low brown plains to Denver, very little settled, and with trails going in all directions. My sailing orders were 'steer south, and keep to the best beaten track,' and it seemed like embarking on the ocean without a compass. The rolling brown waves on which you see a horse a mile and a half off impress one strangely, and at noon the sky darkened up for another storm, the mountains swept down in blackness to the Plains, and the higher peaks took on a ghastly grimness horrid to behold.

In the month Bird spent in the mountains, Jay Cooke and Company, which had underwritten the railroad boom, declared bankruptcy, and banks suspended business in panic. When Bird came back to Denver, she found that she could not cash her traveler's checks. She went on to South Park with little more than her frayed traveling dresses and a fresh horse, and of Denver, she wrote,

> A shooting affray in the street is as rare as in Liverpool, and one no longer sees men dangling to the lampposts when one looks out in the morning! It is a busy place, the entrepot and distributing point for an immense district, with good shops, some factories, fair hotels, and the usual deformities and refinements of civilization. Peltry shops abound, and sportsman, hunter, miner, teamster, emigrant, can be completely rigged out at fifty different stores.

Eight decades later, Jack Kerouac saw in Denver a new beginning. Born in Massachusetts, he had attended Columbia University on a football scholarship, and in New York, he met the people who would make up the Beat Generation, including Neal Cassady. Cassady grew up on Denver's skid rows and struck Kerouac as the wild, crazy, and liberated soul that he wanted to be. When a friend invited Kerouac to San Francisco, he took off west. Denver, to which Cassady had returned and Allen Ginsberg had gravitated, was his first stop on this transcontinental road trip, and in the chaos that Isabella Bird shunned he saw freedom and exhilaration. He hitchhiked from New York, and of his arrival in Denver from Cheyenne, he wrote,

> I got on that hot road, and off I went in a brand-new car driven by a Denver businessman of about thirty-five. He went seventy. I tingled all over; I counted minutes and subtracted miles. Just ahead, over the rolling wheatfields all golden beneath the distant snows of Estes, I'd be seeing old Denver at last. I pictured myself in a Denver bar that night, with all the gang, and in their eyes I would be strange and ragged and like the Prophet who has walked across the land to bring the dark Word, and the only Word I had was "Wow!" The man and I had a long, warm conversation about our respective schemes in life, and before I knew it we were going over the wholesale fruit markets outside Denver; there were smokestacks, smoke, railyards, red-brick buildings, and the distant downtown gray stone buildings, and here I was in Denver. He let me off at Larimer Street. I stumbled along with the most wicked grin of joy in the world, among the old bums and beat cowboys of Larimer Street.

TRAVEL BY TRAIN

In 1862, Abraham Lincoln also signed the Pacific Railway Act, which authorized the federal government to finance the transcontinental railroads. Denver, a mining camp that began in 1858, on the plains thought to be a desert, and six hundred miles from the nearest sizable city, needed the railroad to underpin its economy. The Continental Divide, the ridge in the Rockies that separates the Atlantic and Pacific watersheds, was an obstacle. Edward Berthoud, chief engineer of the Colorado Central Pacific Railroad, determined that the transcontinental railroad could cross the Divide at Berthoud Pass, the saddle between the Front Range and Middle Park. The grades on Berthoud Pass exceeded the maximum grade set by Congress, but Berthoud suggested that the limit was based on outmoded ideas and recommended a narrow-gauge line, which would have required a switch from the standard gauge of the transcontinental railroad. The Union Pacific studied the possibility of Berthoud Pass, but it found that in addition to the steep grades, it would require a long tunnel through the granite, an unjustifiable expense in both time and money. In the winter of 1866, Union Pacific president John Dix wrote to territorial governor John Evans that despite this setback, the railroad would not completely rule out Denver, especially if the city could find a more suitable route.

There were none. It had to be Berthoud Pass. The *Rocky Mountain News* founder and editor William Byers exhorted Coloradans to complete the wagon road over Berthoud Pass to prove its viability to the Union Pacific. He also argued that despite the difficulties of the route, the benefits outweighed the alternatives: it is the shortest and most direct route to the Salt Lake basin, as required by law; it would serve wealthy mining districts and fertile agricultural lands, compared to the barren landscapes in the alternatives; west of Berthoud Pass, the line would be easier and cheaper to build; and a railroad through Denver would capture the burgeoning trade in New Mexico and Arizona, which had become a part of the United States two decades before.

That spring, business and civic leaders, tourists, and onlookers came to Berthoud Pass. A late May blizzard caught a group of merchants and veterans at the pass. A Middle Park rancher found the men three days later, in a state of near-starvation and hypothermia. On their return, they reported, "Berthoud Pass presents no obstacles to the passage of the railroad that has not, in other localities, been overcome." Two weeks later, another party set out to cross Berthoud Pass and back in a day, but their horses sunk into the deep snow and they had to dismount and trudge through the slush. They set up camp once they reached a meadow in Middle Park and collapsed from exhaustion. And they reported that since they made it on foot and horseback, Berthoud Pass was perfectly fine for a railroad.

That July, the Union Pacific finalized the route through the Rockies. Chief engineer Granville Dodge concluded that the high altitude of Berthoud Pass, deep snow, steep grades, and the necessity of building tunnels outweighed any advantages the route could confer and built the line through southern Wyoming.

The *Cheyenne Daily Leader* gloated that Denver would not amount to much; the Union Pacific predicted Denver's demise. John Evans and a cadre of Denver businessmen headed to New York and persuaded investors to finance a railroad from Denver to Cheyenne. Back in Denver, William Byers wrote that Denver had no choice but to build its own railroad and urged the citizenry to pass the proposed bond issue. The citizens passed the bonds, and the investors bought them; the Denver Pacific Railway surveyed a route along the South Platte; citizens volunteered to cut the wood and lay the tracks. The Denver Pacific broke ground in May 1868. The first train from Cheyenne arrived in June 1870. Two months later, the Kansas Pacific, the southern transcontinental route from Kansas City, joined the Denver Pacific. Denver connected itself to the world.

BETRAYALS AND LOYALTIES

Among the first Chinese in Denver were laborers on the railroads. Like in many western cities, they formed their own enclave in the heart of the city, where they had their own grocers, shops, laundries, and opium dens. In Denver, the old Chinatown was centered on Market Street, between Nineteenth and Twenty-Second Streets. In the 1940s, it was razed to make way for the warehouse district. A part of this area was razed again in the 1990s for the ballpark, and the rest became a neighborhood of sports bars and nightclubs. A plaque tells the story of the 1880 Hop Alley riots, and it reads in part,

> On October 31, 1880, in John Asmussen's saloon, located on the 1600 block of Wazee, an argument broke out between two pool-playing Chinese and some intoxicated whites. When the Chinese slipped out of the back door, they were attacked and beaten, beginning Denver's first recorded race riot. About 3,000 people

congregated quickly in the area, shouting 'Stamp out the yellow plague!' Destruction of the Chinese ghetto ensued. Several white residents showed remarkable courage in protecting the Chinese: saloonkeeper James Veatch sheltered refugees, as did gambler Jim Moon and Madam Lizzie Preston, whose girls armed themselves with champagne bottles and high heels to hold the mob at bay. Many were injured, and one Chinese man lost his life. Despite 150 claims totaling over $30,000, no Chinese were ever paid for their property or business losses, nor did this dark day end Denver's struggles with the underlying issues of racial prejudice.

Anti-Chinese sentiment was high in 1880, seven years after the railroad collapse and bank panic. Besides the competition in the tightened labor market, identity in both European and Chinese cultures is derived from the inheritance of an exclusive homeland, and the act of leaving is viewed as a loss and a betrayal. Both the whites and Chinese were immigrants in America and viewed each other with distrust. The whites wanted to see themselves as native to this land, while the Chinese wanted to return to their homelands. Naturalization, the process of gaining citizenship in another nation, implies that only through legal means can a person set down roots and recreate the exclusionary homeland. The 1882 Chinese Exclusion Act denied this right to the Chinese.

The first Japanese in Colorado also came to work on the railroads. The whites regarded them as they did the Chinese—as alien and rootless—and sought their exclusion. On December 7, 1941, the Japanese navy attacked Pearl Harbor, and the Japanese, including those in the United States, officially became the enemy. On February 19, 1942, Franklin Roosevelt signed an executive order that allowed the military to designate exclusion zones, and people of Japanese ancestry, citizens and non-citizens alike, were excluded from the West Coast. Ten days later, Colorado governor Ralph Lawrence Carr invited the Japanese, as well as Germans and Italians, to seek shelter in Colorado. He said, "They are as loyal to American institutions as you and I. Many of them have been born here and are American citizens with no connection with or feeling of loyalty toward the customs and philosophies of Italy, Germany, and Japan."

That year, he narrowly lost his senatorial run, a loss that many political observers attributed to his defense of the rights of Japanese-Americans. Some of his associates suggested that he had developed an acute sense of fairness and justice during his career as an attorney in the rural, poor, and largely Hispanic communities in southern Colorado, and he carried these principles into his political life. Whatever his motivations, the Japanese-American community erected a bust of him in Denver's Sakura Square, with an engraving that reads,

> In the hysteria of World War II, when others in authority forgot the noble principles that make the United States unique, Colorado's governor Ralph L. Carr had the wisdom and courage to speak out on behalf of the persecuted Japanese-American minority. 'They are loyal Americans,' he said, 'sharing only race with the enemy.' He welcomed them to Colorado to take part in the state's war effort. And such were the times that this forthright act may have doomed his political future. Thousands came, seeking refuge from the West Coast's hostility, made new homes and remained to contribute much to Colorado's civic, cultural, and economic life. Those who benefited from Governor Carr's humanity have built their monument in grateful memory of his unflinching Americanism, and as a lasting reminder that the precious democratic ideals he espoused must forever be defended against prejudice and neglect.

THROUGH THE LOOKING GLASS

In September 1870, a *New York Times* correspondent rode into Denver on the Kansas Pacific and wrote of the first sight of the Rocky Mountains, "As the full view of the chain burst upon us suddenly, on reaching the summit of a plateau, the entire party broke forth in shouts of admiration and applause." He alighted near Larimer Street and waxed lyrical on the progress of the nation moving westward, "The country is beautiful and very rich in products, and these towns with their railroad connections, manufactures, wholesale and retail stores, gas-works and handsome improvements of all kinds, each one worthy of a separate chapter, are living, moving exemplifications of the spirit and confidence of the people." The lax morals of the frontier dismayed him though, for he quipped, "Here, in the capital of Colorado, are moral leprosies and reckless heathenisms sufficiently developed to satisfy the most ardent devotee, that great achievements in the Master's name are to be wrought, ere Christian civilization can claim Denver as her own."

Into the twentieth century, as automobiles and airplanes supplanted the passenger train, fewer travelers came through the neighborhood of Larimer Street and the district became a skid row. Neal Cassady grew up here. His parents had separated over his father's alcoholism. Cassady initially lived with his mother and half-siblings, but his mother died when he was ten, and he went to live with his father on Larimer Street. His father worked in a barbershop on Seventeenth and Larimer, but he spent most of his wages on drink and the younger Cassady often ate at soup kitchens. They lived in the residential Metropolitan Hotel on Sixteenth and Market, where the chimes of the Daniels and Fisher department store clock tower woke them at seven each morning.

The department store is no longer there. Neither is the Metropolitan Hotel nor the elder Cassady's barbershop. Sixteenth and Market is now the bus depot at which I alight every morning for work; Seventeenth and Larimer is part of the office district. The clock tower remains, the basement occupied by a cabaret, and I am hardly in the city early enough to hear its chimes. I had come to Denver at the beginning of the twenty-first century, when Larimer Street had become a dining and shopping district anchored by the basketball and hockey arena Pepsi Center and the ballpark Coors Field, the kind of place that is at once everywhere and nowhere, a mecca for leisure and consumption replicated in cities across the world.

One desultory fall afternoon I walked into Union Station, a Beaux-Arts building first built in 1881 to consolidate Denver's four train depots. The waiting area was empty; I sat on a bench and watched the light stream in through the high windows. Nowadays, only two passenger trains come through Union Station each day: the California Zephyr to and from Chicago and the San Francisco Bay Area. The Ski Train to Winter Park, which crosses the Divide into Middle Park at Moffatt Tunnel—Berthoud

Pass is now a highway—closed recently. A year after my visit, the station closed for renovation and it is slated to reopen as a transit center for light and commuter rail. At the station, I heard footsteps in the hall, so quiet that they seemed like ghosts, and it occurred to me then that Denver is itinerant, shaped by restless journeys to the West.

Ascent

ALL THAT MORNING FOG rolled from the mountains to the plains. As I hiked the trail toward Longs Peak, the firs and spruces shrunk from forests to twisted stumps. Near timberline, close to a rushing creek, a sign warned of the dangers of lightning in the alpine tundra. For a moment, I worried that the grey mists were instead storm clouds, that I would have to turn back without reaching my destination, but as I climbed above the trees, the fog lay at my feet and spit into the sky. Before me, the three summits of Mount Meeker, Longs Peak, and Mount Lady Washington sat like monarchs, the sky a blistering blue, the fog around them a moat.

At 14,259 feet, Longs Peak is not the highest point in Colorado. That would be Mount Elbert at 14,440 feet. Longs Peak is a fourteener, a summit above 14,000 feet, and the one most visible from Denver; around here, bagging fourteeners is a sport. There are a number of ways to reach its summit. The Keyhole, the standard hiking route, is a sixteen-mile round trip with nearly a mile of elevation gain. In the summer, the last mile or two is mostly a scramble, but in the spring, it becomes a technical mountaineering route and climbers prefer to ascend the couloirs on the East Face with their ice axes and crampons. The most challenging route is the Diamond on the East Face, a thousand feet of sheer vertical granite above the sparkling waters of Chasm Lake.

In many cultures, the sky is a symbol of heaven. Mountains occupy the liminal space between earth and sky and are thus seen as paths to the divine. In the ninth century, Chinese poet Han Shan sought enlightenment on Cold Mountain. A millennium later in America, John Muir wandered in the Sierra, saw the Yosemite peaks as cathedrals, and fell onto his knees in prayer. A century later, another John, one who took the name of his favorite city as his stage name, sang,

> But the Colorado Rocky Mountain high
> I've seen it rainin' fire in the sky
> Talk to God and listen to the casual reply.

On the other hand, in some parts of the Himalayas, it is considered a sacrilege to climb sacred peaks. Pilgrims circumambulate them instead, a practice of walking prayer that poet Gary Snyder brought to Mount Tamalpais just north of San Francisco.

In Western culture, mountaineering is both a spiritual discipline as well as a mark of ambition and achievement. We associate heights with power. To reach a summit is to reach a pinnacle of power; there is nowhere higher to go, not immediately at least. First ascents, especially of the highest peaks, make history: think of Edmund Hillary and Tenzing Norgay on Everest, Edward Whymper on the Matterhorn. Before a first ascent, a peak is unknown to us. To climb it successfully is also to bring back knowledge of its routes and secrets, to make the unknown known. We repeat climbers' tales of impassable walls, intractable footholds, adverse weather, harrowing descents, near slips, and fatal mistakes until they become the stories by which we define the peak.

"Were not the divinely illuminated passes of [Albert] Bierstadt's Sierra meant to confirm the successful completion of our manifest destiny?" writes Joan Didion of the nineteenth century painter's romanticized depictions of the Rockies and the Sierra. We use the word *virgin* to describe territory that is yet to be discovered by man. I say "man," for the concept is gendered; places, like women, are prized for their purity, and their value is diminished once a man has made incursions into them. To be the first, then, is also to claim this power for yourself. And to call yourself the first is to write a version of this history that erases those who came before you. Needless to say, the majority of explorers and climbers—at least those whose adventures we record and remember—have been white men.

Denver lies where the Great Plains meet the Rockies, at the confluence of Cherry Creek and the South Platte. As I have said, from the city, Longs Peak is the highest visible point. From the right vantage point on a clear day, one can also see Pikes Peak, the fourteener near Colorado Springs a hundred miles south that inspired Katharine Lee Bates to write "America the Beautiful," that hymn to amber waves of grain, purple mountain majesties, and America's destiny to span from sea to shining sea. John Wesley Powell, the one-armed Civil War veteran best known for his harrowing descent of the Grand Canyon, is often said to have made the first ascent on Longs Peak, but it is more accurate to say that he made the first *recorded* ascent.

The Arapaho lived in Colorado before European settlers came, spending their summers in the mountains and winters on the plains. They navigated by the prominence of Longs Peak and Mount Meeker and called them *neniisotoyou'u,* or the Two Guides. In the early twentieth century, a Colorado Mountain Club (CMC) volunteer followed two elderly Arapaho to Longs Peak, trying to record their stories even as he did not understand their language. One of the men told a story of his father trapping eagle feathers on the peak. He might have been deliberately misleading the white man or the CMC volunteer might have misunderstood what he said, but it is likely that the Arapaho had reached the summit before the first whites arrived.

In fact, Longs Peak is named for a man who did not climb it. In the aughts of the nineteenth century, army officer Zebulon Pike led an expedition to find the headwaters of the Arkansas and Red Rivers. His party arrived in the Rockies in the late fall and saw a peak that towered over the landscape. They made an attempt, but they could not get past the ferocious ice and snow even this early in the season. With winter approaching, they abandoned the effort and decided to push on into the Rockies instead. Unprepared for the harsh winter, they lost their bearings and unwittingly crossed into Spanish Mexico. They set up a fort near present-day Alamosa, where Spanish soldiers from Santa Fe arrested them on charges of espionage. As Spain wanted to maintain friendly relations with the United States, they released Pike, a commissioned officer, but many of his men remained in prison.

Two decades later, Major Stephen Long led a survey of the Missouri and Platte Rivers, during which he described the Plains as a great desert unsuitable for civilization. After weeks on a prairie that resembled a sea, with few topographical features to keep them oriented, they must have been both awed and relieved when they saw the unbroken chain of snow-capped peaks that is the Rockies. When they arrived near present-day Denver, they saw a summit that towered over every other and thought it was the peak that Pike had described in his report. Long did not climb it, though it has since been named for him, nor did he realize it was a different summit until they traveled to what is now Colorado Springs and ascended what is now called Pikes Peak.

Denver began as a mining camp in 1859, at the height of the Pikes Peak gold rush, and as the city grew, many men sought to climb Longs Peak. Among these amateur mountaineers was William Byers, the founding editor of the *Rocky Mountain News*. As the owner of Denver's first newspaper, he made it his duty to promote the territory's virtues, often to the point of comic exaggeration. In 1864, he joined a climbing party and made it as far as the Boulder Field on the east side of the peak. From there, they could not find a route and turned back. They likely saw the vertical walls of the Diamond and the crags and couloirs around it; the Keyhole, which to this day is the only known non-technical route to the summit, loops around the west side, not the most intuitive for those seeking the shortest way to the top.

In 1868, John Wesley Powell came to Denver on a reconnaissance trip for the expedition on the Green and Colorado Rivers that would make his name. In Denver, he met Byers. Byers recognized him as a man of ambition, and it was likely he who convinced Powell to make a bid on Longs Peak. The mountain was not part of Powell's plans, but he was intrigued by the possibility of having the first ascent to his name. Byers joined the climb, and it was also likely he who told Powell that the east side was impassable and that they should try from the west. The party crossed Berthoud Pass, which a year before the Union Pacific had rejected as a route for the transcontinental railroad because of the steep grades and snow that lingered into the summer, and they set up a base camp near Grand Lake.

The route that Powell took to the summit of Longs Peak is so arduous and improbable that it is unlikely that anyone has repeated it. The men whacked through brush and forest to timberline. At the Continental Divide, the scree was too rough for their horses. They tied up their animals and labored across the peaks and saddles on foot. They climbed and descended at least five or six peaks between 12,000 and 13,000 feet, many of them also first ascents, and arrived at Pagoda Mountain, a dome-shaped summit just one chasm away from their goal. There, however, they found the trough impossible to cross and descended into the valley now called Wild Basin.

It was too late in the day to try for the peak and the men spent the cold summer night without adequate supplies. The next day, they climbed a couloir on Mount Meeker, which, as Byers later wrote in his account for the *Rocky*, "In many places, it required the assistance of hands as well as feet to get along, and the ascent at best was very laborious." From Mount Meeker, they finally crossed a ridge to Longs Peak. As Byers wrote of standing at the top of this world, "The view was very extensive in all directions: including Pike's Peak, south, the Sawatch Ranges southwest, Gore's Range and the Elkhorn Mountains west, the Medicine Bow and Sweetwater north, and a vast extent of the plains east. Denver was plainly distinguishable to the naked eye."

In the fall of 1873, two women summited Longs Peak on separate occasions. Both were later chided for their inappropriate attire. Then, and more covertly now, men are seen as agents of change, with the freedom to adventure into the unknown, while women are seen as keepers of culture, of the hearth and home. It was not uncommon for wives and daughters to accompany expeditions, and when they did, they often took care of the chores at camp while the men scouted the route ahead. In other words, even on the quest to expand the frontier, they still did the maintenance work and if they had ambitions, they could not outwardly pursue them. Women also joined social hiking clubs and walked the trails in long skirts and petticoats. The solo woman traveler, on the other hand, did not carry the accouterments of home and family. She had to be disciplined for transgressing her role.

Anna Dickinson was an abolitionist and suffragist, a celebrated public speaker, and a veteran of a number of Colorado's fourteeners. In September 1873, she joined Ferdinand Hayden's survey of Longs Peak. The summit had already been reached, and Hayden's task was instead to draw up maps and name the remaining unnamed features. On the climb, Dickinson reportedly discarded her skirts and wore men's trousers, a detail that the local newspapers turned into a minor scandal. She was the only woman in the party to reach the summit. On the way down, the men, suitably impressed, asked her to name the peak next to Longs. She suggested Mount Washington for the New Hampshire peak she often climbed, and in her honor, they named it Mount Lady Washington.

That October, English traveler Isabella Bird arrived in Estes Park. The daughter of a clergyman, Bird was a sickly child. A doctor prescribed travel, and she found that her ailments vanished when she was on the road. She was on the way back to England from the Sandwich Islands, as Hawaii was then called, when she planned to detour into the Rockies. Alighting from the Union Pacific in Cheyenne, she rented a horse and rode from the plains into the mountains. There, she met Jim Nugent, a notorious desperado and fellow countryman. Despite his reputation, she found him congenial and even cultured. They formed a close friendship that might have veered into romance. He offered to show her up Longs Peak.

The two young men who came along saw Bird as a liability and wanted to leave her behind, but Nugent insisted that if not for the lady, he would not be guiding them. They slipped and slid in the ice and snow of late fall. In her letters to her sister, Bird wrote, "You know I have no head and no ankles, and never ought to dream of mountaineering, and had I known that the ascent was a real mountaineering feat I should not have felt the slightest ambition to perform it." Nugent roped her to himself and hauled her to the summit. They ran out of water, and one of the young men suffered a nosebleed, but of the experience, she wrote, "A more successful ascent of the Peak was never made, and I would not now exchange my memories of its perfect beauty and extraordinary sublimity for any other experience of mountaineering in any part of the world."

Back in England, Bird published her letters to her sister as *A Lady's Life in the Rocky Mountains*. A male London critic remarked that she must have worn men's clothes on the climb. Insulted, she insisted that subsequent editions of the book contain a sketch of her wearing an "American lady's mountain dress": a jacket, an ankle-length skirt, and long trousers, an outfit comfortable enough for rough travel and yet still suitably feminine. She might have thrown off the shackles of her gender to roam the world alone, but she still was conscious of her image and propriety. Or maybe this was a Victorian lady's idea of showing the middle finger to her critics. But more than that, it was a triumph for women who wanted to define their own lives on their own terms.

I was not heading to the peak. That day, my goal was Chasm Lake, a gorgeous alpine lake that is a destination in its own right. At the base of the Diamond, the lake's glacial waters glint obsidian when the sun casts shadows from Longs Peak. It is not a peak climb, but the hike is not trivial either; it is long and steep and a scramble in parts. It wraps around a flank of Mount Lady Washington where alpine columbines bloom at the height of summer, their white and purple petals fluttering in the light breeze. Streams too small to name tumble down cliffs and form emerald pools. In any other place, the hike to Chasm Lake would have been the crown jewel of the area, but here it is eclipsed by one of Colorado's most storied peaks.

I reached a fork in the trail and hesitated. The path to the left would take me to Chasm Lake, the right to Longs Peak, and at the back of my mind, I began to calculate whether I could make the summit. The peak often attracts lightning storms and hikers are recommended to start at three in the morning so they can begin their descent before noon, when most summer storms tend to arrive. It was already almost noon, but there was not a cloud in the sky for miles. There were nine more hours to sunset, and I had a headlamp and food in my pack. As I made the calculations, I saw that I was following the story I had been taught about ambition: that we should always take the route to the top, even if it was not in our plans.

The stories I knew of this landscape were of the peak. And there are many other such stories that I have not recounted here, of itinerant mountain guides, fatal winter climbs, and attempts to set records on the Diamond (which is currently at three hours, fifty-three minutes, and fifty-nine seconds car-to-car), but the stories I am most drawn to are of the first ascents, the first claims to knowledge and power in this place where I have chosen to live, the ways we are taught we can make the unknown known. The conditions that day were such that I could have made a late ascent on the peak, limited more by my own abilities than the vagaries of weather in the mountains. I could follow the route that I had been trained to believe I should want.

On some level, I felt I was missing out if I did not take the chance to climb the peak. And yet I already had a different plan, one that was perhaps less glamorous but no less worthy. Mountains, after all, are not just about snow-capped ridges that scrape the sky. There are many other mountain landscapes we can venerate: valleys, meadows, forests, streams, waterfalls, and, of course, alpine lakes, their colors turning cobalt or turquoise as sunlight hits the glacial silt in the water. To walk in these places is a kind of circumambulation; the pace is more measured, more suited for contemplation. In contrast to the adrenaline rush of reaching for the sky, in this liminal space, we can inhabit the present, listen to the rhythms of our bodies, and explore the unknowability within ourselves.

I vowed to return someday and set off on the trail to the lake.

The Ideology of Paradise

THE STANFORD UNIVERSITY CAMPUS is beautiful. Its Mission Revival buildings sprawl under the warm California sky, evoking the haciendas of another era. Palm trees line long walkways across the lawns, evoking space and solitude for rambling and thinking. I knew that the university was founded with robber baron money, acquired through wrecking places and exploiting people. I knew that it is now the academic heart of Silicon Valley and venture capitalism, arguably the modern iteration of the robber barons. I knew better than to think of a place outside of its historical and social context, but as I walked around the campus with a friend— neither of us students and neither of us living in the Bay Area—I could not help but see the grounds as a paradise, a retreat from the quotidian and a sanctuary for art and scholarship.

At that time, I was beginning to write, trying to find the subjects that would enable me to delve into the questions I wanted to ask. And I was squeezing in these attempts at a life of the mind into the interstices of the day, between all my obligations of work and life. I was anxious, harried, and exhausted, from both the mental overload as well as the terrifying uncertainty of whether I was good enough to be a writer. I fantasized about having my own quiet space, walled off from the demands of the world. In this state of mind, as I walked around the campus, I imagined spending my days on these footpaths, the warm air, blue skies, and luxurious grass antidotes to the disembodiment of staring at a screen. This is a place, I said to myself, where we can wrestle with our deepest thoughts. This is a place where ideas are made.

What I saw was the ideal, or perhaps the delusion, of the university as a rarefied space that fosters learning and thinking, apart from the caprices of everyday life. It only states the obvious that any college— not just Stanford—is not unaffected by the world around it, be it the skyrocketing cost of tuition that makes access unaffordable to many or the rocky town-gown relations in many college towns. But Stanford in particular, with its massive courtyards, the Rodin sculpture garden, and the Romanesque arches on the central plaza, among other things, feels elevated, designed to be separate. Paradise may be the highest ideal of a culture's imagination, but it is created with wealth and power, with all of the attendant compromises.

The wealth that built this campus belonged to Amasa Leland Stanford, president and one of the original four investors of the Central Pacific Railroad. Stanford grew up near Albany in central New York and trained as a lawyer, but when a fire destroyed his Wisconsin office in 1852, he followed his brothers west. Those were the years of the California gold rush, but he was astute enough not to take his chances as a miner. Instead, he became a merchant in the camps, making his money by provisioning the fools who dreamed of gold. In 1861, when Congress was planning to authorize the financing of a railroad across the untrammeled expanses of the West, Stanford—together with Mark Hopkins, Charles Crocker, and Collis Huntington—put his money into the nascent Central Pacific.

The Central Pacific made Stanford one of the richest men of his time, in large part due to his fluency in mixing business and politics for personal gain. He was also the governor of California from 1862 to 1863, during which time he gave favorable contracts to his railroad cronies. He made the city and county of San Francisco pay for the tracks from the Central Pacific's terminus in Sacramento to San Francisco, while the profits from the operation went to the railroad. He falsely classified the flat desert lands just west of the Sierra as mountain grades and claimed the higher rate of subsidy from the federal government. And together with the Union Pacific, the two railroads argued in court that they should not need to pay back the combined $50 million loan they took from the Treasury in 1862 to finance the first transcontinental railroad.

Stanford's son and only child Leland Stanford Jr. was born when he was forty-four, after his wife Jane suffered a number of miscarriages. He raised the boy to be a steward of wealth and to look to Europe, instead of the young American nation or worse, the empty spaces of the West, as the crucible of culture. In 1884, when the boy was fifteen, Stanford and Jane brought their son on a Grand Tour of Europe, as was common for many aristocratic young European men at the time. The boy, however, contracted typhoid on the trip. He hovered between life and death for a few weeks before he succumbed in Italy, a few months short of his sixteenth birthday. Devastated, and bereft of an heir, Stanford told Jane, "The children of California shall be our children." In this spirit, they decided to found a university in their son's memory on their Palo Alto ranch.

The Leland Stanford Junior University was inaugurated in 1891. Stanford modeled the institution after Harvard and hired away most of the initial fifteen faculty members from Indiana University and Cornell. The university did not charge tuition, which made it affordable to the poor and working class. It was also co-educational, uncommon in those times, though Jane Stanford instituted a quota for women, believing that a women's college did not befit her son's memory. The curriculum focused on the practical arts and sciences, the knowledge with which graduates could go out into the world as innovators and entrepreneurs. Among the students in the first matriculating class was Herbert Hoover, an orphan from Iowa. He graduated with a degree in geology, worked as a mining engineer, and in 1929, he became the president of the United States.

How do we reconcile art and beauty in the face of vicarious greed? This was the question on my mind as we wandered our way toward the Memorial Church, the crown jewel at the heart of the campus. At the entrance, above the stained glass, a mosaic depicted the Sermon on the Mount. The disciples and followers were dressed in brightly colored robes, their faces turned, their hands raised to Jesus. Palm trees dotted the background. The sky was inlaid with gold leaf. Inside the church, there were more stained glass, mosaics, and marble sculptures; Jane Stanford had a

Victorian aversion to blank space and had filled almost every available spot in the church with art. The effect was grandiose and overwhelming, as though meant to compensate for emptiness elsewhere, but still, in the church, I saw a sacred space that was dedicated to matters of the spirit.

The Memorial Church was among the last of the original structures of the campus to be built. The Stanfords believed that the education of the spirit was integral to the education of the mind, and to that end, they envisioned a non-denominational church on the Main Quad, the plaza at the center of the campus. Stanford died in 1893, before the church was built. That year, the nation was deep in a recession caused by railroad speculation and a run on the gold supply. Two years later, the federal government sued the Stanford estate for the repayment of the loan it had made to the Central Pacific to build the original road. With a thirty-year maturity and an interest rate of 6 percent—none of it paid—the railroad owed more than $63 million, not counting any late interest, due in 1892. The lawsuit froze the estate's assets and threatened the continued operation of the university.

Jane Stanford, until then a housewife, took over the university administration and steered it through these difficult years. She paid salaries and expenses out of her own pocket and by pawning her jewelry. For thirty years, the two railroads had been arguing before the courts over the date on which the first transcontinental railroad was completed, the definition of net earnings, and other legal technicalities to avoid paying back the loan; the federal government's case went all the way to the US Supreme Court and was ultimately settled in favor of the Stanford estate. The money now freed, Jane began planning and designing the church. Before her husband died, they had traveled to Europe for inspiration; the final design resembled the medieval churches they saw in Italy. The Memorial Church was completed in 1903 and dedicated to Leland's memory.

Next to the entrance of the Memorial Church, I saw this inscription on the wall:

> There is no narrowing so deadly as the narrowing of man's horizon of spiritual things. No worse evil could befall him in his course on earth than to lose sight of heaven. And it is not civilization that

can prevent this; it is not civilization that can compensate for it. No widening of science, no possession of abstract truth, can indemnify for an enfeebled hold on the highest and central truths of humanity. "What shall a man give in exchange for his soul?"

The sentiment is noble, even if it reads like a Victorian idea of a motivational quote, a platitude that sounds deep on the surface but ultimately comes up empty. But I also saw that it echoed my aspirations as a writer to transcend the materiality of everyday life in search of a higher truth. I did not know how to say it even to myself then, but I wanted a heaven, a paradise, made from words and ideas that cut to the truth of my lived experiences. I knew, on some level, that I needed to develop an inner compass to navigate the world and that, to do so, I needed to look beyond the demands of my day-to-day existence and figure out what I believed and valued.

But I also chuckled, for it is precisely the unfettered capitalism the robber barons fostered that takes us away from this noble work of the spirit. And I thought of the 2010 US Supreme Court case *Citizens United v. Federal Election Commission,* in which the court ruled that to restrict corporate spending on electoral campaigns violated corporations' free speech rights under the First Amendment. The ruling hinged on corporate personhood, a legal concept that the court first established in the 1886 decision *Santa Clara County v. Southern Pacific Railroad.* The Southern Pacific, successor to the Central Pacific and of which Stanford was president at the time, argued that the tax the Santa Clara County sued them to collect, which applied to railroads and not natural persons, amounted to differential treatment, a violation of their equal rights under the Fourteenth Amendment. The high court ruled in favor of the railroad, but it would have been just a minor tax dispute if it had not also reached, at the railroad's behest, to assert that corporations had the same rights as natural persons.

The Southern Pacific was known as the Octopus, for its many tentacles reached far and wide across American society, from the networks of freight lines to the influence of business on politics. In many ways, it was a pioneer of the modern corporation, with all its excesses and abuses. With the *Citizens United* decision, these slippery arms also reached into the present, opening the gates to virtually unlimited corporate spending on electoral politics. More than that, it conflated money with speech, making voices that are not aligned with the interests of wealth and power difficult to be heard, if not dismissed outright. To put it another way, this decision enfeebled our hold on the highest and central truths of humanity, the free exchange of speech that is at the center of art and knowledge, and narrowed our horizon of spiritual things to that which upholds the ideology of dominance. In this context, heaven is the selling of our deepest beliefs and values to the highest bidder.

Like most people, Stanford was a complex man. He was one of the most ruthless businessmen of his time, but he also founded a great institution that continues to advance our knowledge of the arts and sciences and ultimately of the human condition. It is easy to be cynical and say that he used his philanthropy to soften his image—after all, more than a century after his death, more people associate the name Stanford with the university than the Central Pacific, if they even know the history of the railroad. But it is not an either/or proposition: both the university, in all of its academic glory, and the railroad, in all of its splendorous corruption, are his legacies. Looked at this way, these twin legacies leave us with questions: What lies beneath our dreams of paradise? What shall a man give in exchange for his soul?

A Memory of Hills

ON APRIL 20, 1914, the Colorado National Guard opened fire on a tent colony of 1,200 striking coal miners in the southern Rockies, killing between nineteen and twenty-five people, including camp leader Louis Tikas, and wounding many more. In the months before that Easter Monday, the miners and their families dug pits under the tents to hide from bullets. On the day after the bloodshed, four women and eleven children were found huddled in a pit. All but two of the women suffocated when the tent above them caught fire.

At the turn of the twentieth century, Colorado's coalfields resembled feudal towns. Miners were paid by tonnage, that is, the amount of coal they hauled each day. The company men who weighed the coal often lowered their measurements to pay the miners less. Dead work like building structural reinforcements and laying track went unpaid. Many miners, desperate to make a living wage, took safety shortcuts. As a result, the death toll in Colorado's mines was twice the national average. Miners also lived in company towns where guards watched their every move and they were often paid in scrip.

The coal companies tried to suppress union activities. Despite this, the United Mine Workers of America (or UMWA) secretly organized the miners, and in 1913, it presented a list of demands, which included recognition of the union, a pay raise, payment for dead work, abolition of scrip and company towns, worker election of weightmen, and an eight-hour workday. The companies rejected them, and that September, the miners went on strike. Evicted from their company houses, they set up camps at the mouths of the canyons leading to the mines.

The Colorado Fuel & Iron Company (or CF&I), which owned most of these mines, hired the Baldwin-Felts Detective Agency to break the strike. Baldwin-Felts brought in what the miners called the Death Special, an armored car outfitted with machine guns that peppered bullets into the tents. The state sent in the Colorado National Guard to maintain order, but as the brutal winter turned into spring, it could no longer afford to pay them. Governor Elias Ammons withdrew all but two of the units and allowed the CF&I to finance a militia in guard uniform.

The day after Easter, three guards arrived at the camp, demanding the release of a man they claimed the strikers held captive. Louis Tikas went to the train depot half a mile away to negotiate with the militia leader. Once he left, a gunfight broke out between the militia and the strikers. Many miners and their families fled to the mountains. Three miners, including Tikas, were shot dead and their bodies left along the railway tracks for three days. After the UMWA found the bodies in the pit, it launched a guerilla war. The violence lasted ten more days and claimed fifty more lives, quelled only when Woodrow Wilson sent in federal troops. The Ludlow Massacre is often considered the most violent labor conflict in American history.

*

I wonder about John D. Rockefeller Jr., the only son and heir of the Standard Oil industrialist John D. Rockefeller and the controlling stakeholder of the CF&I at the time of the massacre. It is easy to vilify him as a heartless capitalist bent on profits at the cost of lives, but I think it is more insidious than that. His father believed that employing workers was an act of charity and in 1915 testified before Congress that even if he knew the company guards were shooting at miners, he would not have stopped them. On the other hand, Ludlow seemed to have impinged on Junior's conscience; he visited the coalfields, met with survivors, and worked to improve labor relations.

By most accounts, Junior was a family man devoted to his wife Abby Aldrich until her death, a strict but doting father to their six children, and a dutiful son to the father in whose shadow he lived. He was also a philanthropist; the year *before* the massacre, he established the Rockefeller Foundation, which funded, among other things, art, medical research, and conservation. In 1910, he resigned as a director of both Standard Oil and US Steel when the companies were embroiled in a corruption scandal. It appears that at his best, he tried to live by the principles of service and fairness.

He inherited his stake in the CF&I from his father. This reliance meant that whatever his convictions might have been, he ultimately had to abide by his father's values. It is unclear whether he directly ordered the militia to shoot the strikers, but he certainly knew about the agitation in southern Colorado, and even though he had the power to stop the brutality, he did not use it. Though he was the largest shareholder of the company, he believed in letting management make decisions with little to no interference. He also believed that collective bargaining hindered rather than improved the workingman's lot, and to that end, he left the managers to deal with the union as they saw fit.

That is to say, as the scion of one of the most powerful men of his time, Rockefeller Jr. inherited an unquestioned privilege that made him blind to the suffering of others. This failure of empathy and imagination led directly to the violence of the Ludlow Massacre.

*

"These are the facts, but facts are not the story," writes David Mason, now the Colorado Poet Laureate, in the verse-novel *Ludlow*. Mason sees the massacre as his inheritance; his family goes back four or five generations in southern Colorado, shopkeepers in Trinidad, a town about twelve miles from the encampment. His grandparents are buried seventy-five yards from Louis Tikas. He grew up listening to his grandfather and uncles talk about Ludlow. On road trips to visit family in Trinidad, his father would point out the scrubby hills from which the militia fired on the miners. He began to write the story when he imagined the orphan Luisa Mole.

Luisa lost her Mexican mother to typhoid when she was very young
and her Welsh father to a mine accident when she was twelve. As her
father no longer works for the CF&I, it evicts her from the company
house. The shopkeeper George Reed and his wife Sarah take her in.
Though they are kind to her, she never becomes part of the family. Her
days are spent on chores and helping at the store. And as the tensions
between the company and the miners escalate, she is torn between her
gratitude toward the Reeds and her loyalties to her people:

Torn in two

by what she saw both far and near, outside
herself and deep inside, as if to witness
feelings she could never speak aloud,
Luisa knew that something of herself
was gypsy and untouchable and never
to be saved.

At the same time, Ilias Spantidakis flees a Crete destroyed by war.
Renamed Louis Tikas by inspectors on Ellis Island, he finds himself hus-
tling for scraps in Denver. The American dream eludes him. Desperate,
he becomes a scab, hired to break strikes in the Frederick mines just north
of Denver. The work

made Louis scream
inside, but like the other men who worked
shoulder to shoulder with him in the seam,

he seldom spoke, afraid to show his fear.

Frustrated by the conditions, he convinces his fellow Greeks to walk out.
The UMWA leader John Lawson is impressed and hires him as a local
organizer.

Mason's characters, whether fictional or based on real people, have
their dreams and fears, ambitions and failures. The Reeds see the strikers
as threats to their security; Luisa feels she has to hide her loyalties from

them. The miners seek a life of dignity; Tikas finds his purpose in organizing. The militia leader Karl Linderfelt lusts for blood; Rockefeller Jr. prizes abstract principles over the realities on the ground. "I believe that the poet shall once again be a maker," Mason quotes Jorge Luis Borges. "I mean, he will tell a story and he will also sing it." In fictionalizing this story in verse, Mason draws out the interiority of the people whose lives clashed in the coalfield wars. He reminds us that history is more than just facts; it has ramifications on our lives.

*

I think of *Ludlow* each time I drive past the Ludlow exit on Interstate 25 between Denver and Santa Fe. The high plains are green in the spring and golden in the fall, and in the distance, the foothills of the Rockies stagger toward the sky. Washes carry trickles of water across the land. White plumes billow from smokestacks in Pueblo and Trinidad. It occurs to me now that I have not taken the detour to visit the old tent colony site, where the UMWA built a monument to honor the victims of the massacre. I'll make it someday, I tell myself. I'll see the landscape in which this story is rooted. In the meantime, I dwell in Mason's poetry,

a vision of the camps in simple words,
a scrap of song, a memory of hills.

At the Ponds

WALDEN PONDS, BOULDER, COLORADO—I AM not much of a bird-watcher, but each time I visit these ponds on the prairie east of the city, I follow the birds: the mallards and loons bobbing on the marshes and dipping their heads into the cold blue water, the flocks of Canada geese flying in aerial formation, the brown plumage of a killdeer lifted to reveal the black stripes on its white breast.

Adjacent to the ponds is the city wastewater treatment plant and mounds of excavated soil behind a wire mesh fence. In winter afternoons, the Rockies to the west are backlit by the sun. Their blue silhouettes deepen as the earth folds toward the sky, and clouds sink around the peaks. Smoke billows from nearby smokestacks. Small planes depart and land at the nearby municipal airport. Abandoned railroad tracks lie just south of the ponds. The ponds were once abandoned gravel pits.

Initially, this land was open prairie. In the 1950s, the ground was mined for gravel, and when the company left, groundwater fluctuated in the pits. In 1967, Boulder voters approved a dedicated sales tax to fund the acquisition and maintenance of open space. In 1974, the county, under the auspices of the open space program, reclaimed the pits as wetlands. Volunteers built dikes, which stemmed the flow of water away from the pits and allowed them to fill up as ponds. They stocked the ponds with fish. They reseeded the ground and planted trees. The cottonwoods established on their own. And the birds came.

An early county planning report for Walden Ponds says,

> Nature must become part of people's daily lives. It cannot function as just a backdrop for entertainment and recreation, however. People need to see themselves as part of a natural community, and this can only happen when there are natural areas, miniature wild areas close to their homes.

It continues,

> Here they should not find more recreational structures and facilities to add to their already over-structured lives, but the peace and harmony of a natural area offering both relaxation and stimulation ... Here the public should be able to find quiet, creative entertainment: nature trails to lead them, undetected, to bird nests and beds of wildflowers, quiet pools of water filled with fish and birds. They should be able to leave their bicycles and cars behind and walk or simply sit and observe.

The report is titled *A Nature Area for Boulder County: A Pilot Surface Mining Project.* In it, the ponds are referred to as the Boulder County Gravel Pits. The introduction quotes Thoreau, "In wildness is the preservation of the world" and mistakenly attributes it to his masterpiece *Walden.* (It appears in his essay "Walking.") Thoreau's sojourn on the shores of Walden Pond in Massachusetts in the 1840s is likely the allusion behind the name Walden Ponds. Like these diked gravel pits, Thoreau's pond was at the edge of town, the woods populated with hunters, woodcutters, runaway slaves, and visitors. More than once Thoreau remarked on the railroad that cut nearby. He lamented the acceleration and regimentation the railroad would bring, but he also used its exact schedule as a timekeeper and its tracks as a conveyance into town.

I had resisted reading *Walden* for years, as I had thought it was simply a collection of sentimental nature reveries, the musings of an unencumbered white man who had the privilege to isolate himself from society. In the introduction to the Beacon Press edition that I eventually bought, environmental writer Bill McKibben casts Thoreau's material simplicity as a spiritual guide for our consumerist times. Activist and essayist Rebecca Solnit, who found her voice as a writer in the anti-nuclear demonstrations at the Nevada Test Site, finds radical politics in Thoreau's woods, from his helping of runaway slaves to the pleasures of huckleberrying after a night in jail. When I finally read *Walden,* I found that this spirituality and politics are joined by a deep trust in direct observation and the individual experience.

Thoreau begins *Walden* with a discussion on personal economics. His asceticism is extreme for most—he slept on a wooden bed, wore the same frayed clothes, and ate mostly rye and Indian bread—but he rightly argues that material pursuits distract us from the pleasures of the mind. The book may seem to be an interminable litany of long walks, animals in the woods, ice on the pond, and colonies of ants at war, but in observing nature, Thoreau cultivates trust in the individual conscience. Midway in his sojourn at the pond, he went into the village to get his shoes mended and met the tax collector, who threw him into jail for not paying the poll tax. His aunt bailed him out the next day. Thoreau had not paid the poll tax as he opposed the war on Mexico and the government's complicity with slavery; he continued to pay the highway tax as he wanted the roads kept open. For Thoreau, his self-imposed seclusion in nature was about connection rather than isolation; it gave him the space to engage with the social and political issues of his time.

The year after he left Walden Pond, he delivered the lectures at the Concord Lyceum that formed the basis of his essay *Civil Disobedience,* in which he argues that the individual conscience holds moral authority over unjust systems of power. Neither slavery nor the Mexican war directly affected Thoreau, a white man in Massachusetts, but both impinged on his conscience. His act of resistance did not directly end slavery or the war, but it influenced two influential men of the twentieth century. Indian independence leader Mohandas Gandhi promoted the spinning wheel as a way for India to become self-sufficient, boycott British goods, and thus protest the British control of India without violence. American Civil Rights leader Martin Luther King Jr. read Thoreau and Gandhi as a college student and became intrigued by the idea of nonviolent resistance to injustice. King later wrote that as a result of Thoreau's "writings and personal witness, we're heirs to a legacy of creative protest" and that the sit-ins, freedom rides, and Montgomery bus boycott were "outgrowths of Thoreau's insistence that evil must be resisted and that no moral man can patiently adjust to injustice."

I came to Walden Ponds the day after a spring snowstorm. I had just returned from a camping trip in the red rock deserts of Utah, and I wanted to stay close to home. At that time the human world felt capricious, and I sought solace in nature instead. In nature, be it the spectacular landscapes of the American West or these miniature wild areas close to home, I was trying to teach myself to describe the birds and grasses and quality of light, to find the right words for what I could plainly see for myself. I was learning to trust myself after a life of being told that I was not credible, that I was not a reliable witness of my own life, and I sensed that the crucial first step in this journey was to hone my powers of observation.

On that day, despite the ongoing drought, Cottonwood Marsh was a light blue that reflected depth in the water. Herons perched on islands of sand and soil. I followed the boardwalks across the marsh, listening to the high-pitched cries from the cattails. A red-winged blackbird flitted across the reeds, dry and brown this early in the spring. A yellow-headed blackbird flew away, and the red-winged blackbird swooped in to take its spot. Birds fascinate me; they are hard to pin down, always fluttering or on the verge of flight, and yet I can tell where I am from looking at the birds around me. "Red-winged blackbird," an elderly man with a professional camera remarked. "Trying to mark its territory. There aren't many around because of the storm. Come back in a week or two, and you'll see birds everywhere."

I stepped off the boardwalk and walked amid the blue grama and buffalo grass, which, like the reeds, are also dry and brown. It was quiet; I heard only the rustle of grass. A flock of robins suddenly emerged from the grass, like a spray of water from a hose, and they scattered onto the cottonwoods on which first buds had just begun to show. I must have unknowingly trodden into their territory. "It is remarkable how many creatures live wild and free though secret in the woods, and still sustain themselves in the neighborhood of towns," Thoreau wrote of the phoebes and robins by his pond. Beyond my ponds, the ethos of getting and spending that Thoreau decried had culminated in a housing meltdown, a stock market crash, and massive bank bailouts.

It was an ordinary walk around an ordinary pond in my backyard. I did not come to a grand epiphany or combat injustice. But for a couple of hours, I found a space of my own where I could leave the agonies of everyday life behind and be present with the birds. I could wander in this wild community and simply observe. The ideas came later. That afternoon in the marshes, as I put one footstep before another, I learned to trust that the ground would not sink beneath my feet.

III

Visions of Land

The Road Home: On Christo and Jeanne-Claude's *Over the River*

THE ARKANSAS RIVER begins high on the Continental Divide in Colorado's Sawatch Range. It ripples across the alpine tundra, braiding with ice in the winter, watering tufts of columbines in the summer. Gathering water from its tributaries, it enters the Arkansas River valley before spilling onto the Great Plains.

Enter the New York artist Christo. He wants to drape 5.9 miles of silvery fabric over a forty-two mile stretch of the Arkansas River in the Bighorn Sheep Canyon, a project he calls *Over the River.* He and his late wife Jeanne-Claude, who died of a brain aneurysm in 2009, are known for their large-scale wrapping projects such as *The Gates,* in which they hung 7,503 panels of saffron fabric in New York's Central Park for two weeks. He is now seventy-seven. Because of his age, many think that *Over the River,* if it happens, would be his last major artwork. He and Jeanne-Claude first dreamed of it in 1985, when they watched a crew lift the cloth with which they wrapped the Pont-Neuf on the Seine. They imagined a cloth hanging over a river, rippling in the wind and illuminating the light and clouds. From the top, the fibers would appear opaque and reflect the sky.

In 2011, twenty-six years after Christo and Jeanne-Claude first conceived *Over the River,* the Bureau of Land Management (BLM), which oversees most of the land, approved the project. In response, the citizens'

group Rags Over the Arkansas River (ROAR) filed a lawsuit against
BLM. ROAR is also suing the Colorado State Parks for allowing the
project on land it co-manages with BLM. Christo has put the installation
on hold until these cases are settled.

Like most of his projects, Christo has worked on *Over the River* for
decades. Between 1992 and 1994, he, Jeanne-Claude, and two collab-
orators drove around the Rockies in search of a river. They wanted one
with high enough banks to support anchors for the fabric, an east-west
orientation to align the fabric with the arc of the sun, a road for installation and viewing, near a major town for the same reasons, and white
and calm waters for boating and fishing. Many streams in the Rockies
might have fit, but the artists also came here for the headwaters. After
14,000 miles on the road, they settled on six possibilities between Idaho
and New Mexico. They made preliminary measurements at each site and
decided on the Arkansas.

The plan calls for suspending the fabric horizontally above the river,
clear of the banks, using a system of steel wire cables and anchors. Where
the rock is loose, steel caissons would be drilled into the ground with
hydraulic rigs. The artists estimate two springs and two falls for the installation, dodging the winter cold, the summer tourist crush, and the bighorn sheep lambing and raptor nesting seasons. The art would be dis-
played for two weeks in the summer, free to the public. Then all the
components except for the caissons would be taken down and industrially
recycled. This dismantling would take a year.

Over the River is financed entirely by Christo and Jeanne-Claude
through the sale of, among other things, their own preparatory drawings for the project. They do not accept any kind of sponsorship as they
say that the attached strings would interfere with their artistic freedom.
In addition, their works would come at no cost to the host cities. In fall
2010, the Museum of Contemporary Art Denver exhibited some of these
drawings. The canvases are blue and grey in pencil, charcoal, enamel, and
wax, works of art in and of themselves. Blue represents sky and water,
grey the rocks and roads, and the fabric both, a mediation between earth
and sky. Some of the drawings are sketched onto photographs of the
landscape, some collaged with technical specifications for the anchors

and caissons, topographical studies of the river, and fabric samples. These pieces outline a compelling vision of light and form in the Rockies.

As the project is to be largely on public land, the artists sought permits from an array of public agencies, including the Colorado Department of Wildlife, Arkansas Headwaters Recreation Area, Chaffee and Fremont Counties, the Colorado Department of Transportation, and BLM. They also held public meetings in the towns along the river—Salida, Cotopaxi, Cañon City, and many more too small to incorporate. The decision ultimately came down to BLM, the highest of these authorities. In 2006, it requested that because of the complexity of the project, the ongoing environmental assessment had to be upgraded to the more comprehensive environmental impact statement (EIS), a level of study usually done for tunnels and dams. In 2007, the artists submitted a 2,000-page Design and Planning Report to BLM.

In summer 2010, a few months after Jeanne-Claude passed away, BLM issued its draft EIS. It identified problems with erosion, river sedimentation, and rock instability. The drilling would create atypical stresses for the wildlife in the canyon, particularly a threatened native bighorn sheep population. The construction would take place along Highway 50, the main road through the canyon, and cause disruptions for the people who live along the river. BLM was also concerned about the durability of the project in the anomalous wind and hail conditions possible in the summer and the threat to public safety in the event of a collapse. In 1972, a strong gust had torn down Christo's *Valley Curtain,* an orange drape across the Rifle Gap in the central Colorado mountains, and in 1991, high winds toppled one of *The Umbrellas,* a simultaneous installation of blue and yellow umbrellas in Japan and southern California, causing injuries and one fatality. The report also assessed seven alternatives, which range from allowing only paid visitors to view the art to reducing it to just over a mile.

After a public comment period, BLM issued its final EIS in July 2011 and the Record of Decision that November, five months later than initially anticipated. While BLM concluded that *Over the River* would likely have adverse consequences on the river environs and communities, it approved Christo and Jeanne-Claude's original vision, provided that

Christo implements measures to mitigate the impacts. Because the decision came later than scheduled, Christo postponed the viewing period from August 2014 to August 2015.

Christo's vision for the Arkansas River is provocative. The natural world in its untouched state is not necessarily higher than the human imagination. *Over the River* would likely make us see the mountains and rivers in a new light. The fabric would realign our perceptions of depth and space. The work may be temporary, but it would live on in our imaginations, subject to the vagaries of memory. In *The Gates* and *The Pont Neuf Wrapped,* Christo imposed his interpretations on Central Park and the Seine respectively, but New York and Paris are his homes. And the impact of these two works on the environment and residents was minimal. The locals on the Arkansas River argue that *Over the River* is antithetical to the ethos of a rural valley and its allure does not justify its destructions and disruptions.

In February 2012, a group of environmental law students at the University of Denver, under the guidance of their professor Mike Harris, filed a federal lawsuit against BLM on behalf of ROAR. They charge that BLM violated environmental laws in the final EIS. They liken *Over the River* to a mining operation and contend that the agency mischaracterized it as "recreation" and its impact to the river environs as "temporary." The art, they claim, with its drilling operations to install the anchors and caissons, is actually "akin to a massive resource extraction project", its effects on the land and its ecosystems irreversible. In their view, the industrial scale of *Over the River* is not permitted in the land use plans for the area and would unnecessarily degrade the site.

BLM, on behalf of Christo, filed a motion to dismiss the lawsuit. In July, US District Judge John Kane upheld the case. He also put it on hold; a third party not associated with ROAR had filed an appeal against *Over the River* with the Department of the Interior, and Kane would hear the case only after this appeal is resolved. Because of the uncertain time frame, Christo announced that the project would be indefinitely delayed. In September, Kane ruled that Christo cannot start construction on *Over the River* until the case is resolved and that he could join BLM as a defendant on it.

ROAR is based in Cañon City. According to the organization's web-site, its founder is the local businessman Dan Ainsworth. He started the volunteer fire department in his neighborhood and is a former long-distance truck driver. He draws on his experiences fighting wildfires along the Arkansas River and trucking on narrow mountain roads to conclude that *Over the River* would be an environmental and economic disaster. The other members of the Board of Directors include Ainsworth's wife (who is also the bookkeeper), a plant ecologist, an oil field worker and ambulance volunteer, an occupational therapist, and a retired geophysi-cist. The advisors include a fly-fishing guide, a retired Division of Wildlife biologist, and a former National Park Service spokesperson.

ROAR is the most vocal opponent of *Over the River*. They vow to stop it entirely. Their concerns range from the impact on the bighorn sheep population to river erosion, but their central issue is the traffic on Highway 50 for the duration of the project. They emphasize that it is a three-year process of installation, viewing, and removal. Highway 50 is the main road between Salida and Cañon City and the only maintained route through Bighorn Sheep Canyon. The locals use it to access school, work, the grocery store, medical appointments, and their mail. It is also a major truck delivery and ambulance route. The shortest alternative road would add a hundred miles to the journey.

ROAR also charges that contrary to Christo's claims, the drilling rigs would take up both lanes of the narrow canyon road, perpetuating delays counted in hours instead of minutes. These delays could obstruct the response to wildfires and accidents, with potentially fatal results.

Christo's response to this criticism focuses on the two-week viewing period, when thousands of visitors are expected to navigate the winding road while looking at the art. He proposes ambulances and helicopters on standby and alternative routes. For the installation and removal, they would work on the roadside of the canyon only during the tourist off-season. In an early interview, the artists observed that the federal and state agencies are generally supportive of the project while the locals "hate us." Jeanne-Claude in fact said that she had no qualms if the art disrupted the locals on the way to trivial matters like work. Some of ROAR's rhet-oric veers toward hyperbole, such as that the project would cause rock instability and thus earthquakes, but their frustrations are summed up in another of their remarks: "Why is there absolutely no mention of the impact on the local population?"

Christo and Jeanne-Claude's oeuvre belongs to the tradition of land and environmental art, a movement that began in the 1960s, as artists broke out of the museum and gallery system and engaged with public space. *Over the River* has the monumental scale of architecture and sculpture and the impermanence of gesture. Because the work is evanescent, the land appears to be returned to the same condition, as though the art had never been there. The exhibition catalog describes this opus as "gentle disturbances between earth and sky" and "a dialogue between forethought and memory."

That is to say, positive criticism of *Over the River* tends to exalt the aesthetic experience. Museums and galleries have their own politics, but the space is meant to showcase art. In moving to a public space, however, artists have to also contend with competing local uses, which in this case include that of a narrow mountain highway. Public spaces are also encoded with meanings that may not be apparent to artists who encounter them as outsiders. The Arkansas River is a popular recreational site, and many in Colorado seek nature as a respite from the pressures of work and life. An industrial-scale project such as *Over the River* is anathema to this concept of nature. Jeanne-Claude has said, "We want to create works of art of joy and beauty." In other words, she viewed the landscape as akin to the white walls of a museum, without history or memory. The locals were invisible to her.

The opposition to *Over the River* focuses mostly on practical matters, but the implicit sentiment can be read from a river guide's remark that the project is tantamount to "hanging pornography in a church." Behind this hyperbole is a largely American belief, stemming from transcendentalists such as Emerson and Thoreau, in the sanctity of nature. The Arkansas River Valley is surrounded by mountains that hold snow even into the summer, but with its density of communities, abandoned railroad tracks, highways, dams, mine tailings, and recreational outfitters, it is hardly the pristine wilderness that rhapsodists from John Muir to John Denver likened to cathedrals. To the locals, it is home. Their lives and livelihoods depend on the health of the river environs and the local economies. *Over the River* would disrupt their lives for a good part of three years, and when they aired their concerns, Christo and Jeanne-Claude dismissed them. Fairly or not, the residents see the artists as violating the sanctity of their homes.

Christo and Jeanne-Claude are far from the first artists who look to the American West as a setting for their site-specific earthworks. Among the best known are Robert Smithson's *Spiral Jetty* (1970), a sculpture that involved moving almost 7,000 tons of rock and earth on the banks of Utah's Great Salt Lake, Nancy Holt's *Sun Tunnels* (1976), an arrangement of four concrete tunnels in the Great Basin Desert of Nevada, and Walter De Maria's *Lightning Field* (1977), a grid of stainless-steel poles in a desert plateau in west-central New Mexico. These landscapes were chosen for the surreal light and form rarely seen elsewhere, certainly not on the East Coast where all three artists lived; Smithson chose the Great Salt Lake in part for the blood-red color of its water, a phenomenon created by the bacteria and algae that thrive in extreme salinities seen only in deserts. These stark landscapes further enhance the mystique in these works, creating a sense of daring and adventure.

That is to say, these land artists of the 1970s bought into the myth of the American West as a stage for their ambitions and a blank slate on which they could impose their own visions. As much as their work has endured and continues to invite dialogue on the nature of art and imagination, they did not question the founding ethos of the West as an empty space for pushing boundaries of the known, which conveniently erases the people who actually live here. Christo and Jeanne-Claude may claim that they are not land artists as their works are only temporary, but in the proposal for *Over the River,* they continue this tradition of interrogating the aesthetics of the landscape and ignoring the existing stories of the place. Their work belies an arrogance that privileges their ingenuity over the realities on the ground, even if these ideas are draped in the gentility of art.

If Christo and Jeanne-Claude had proposed a massive earthwork that would disrupt access to a ritzy resort town such as Aspen, it would likely have been a nonstarter. The residents, including the second-home owners who live there part-time, would be up in arms, and they have the clout to put a stop to the project. Highway 82, the only road through Aspen, the east side of which—Independence Pass—is closed in the winter as the high mountain pass is difficult to plow, has many of the same features that drew the artists to Highway 50. But it is likely that they did not even think to consider the site as they knew on some level that it would be impossible to push it past the residents. To look at it more cynically, the artists would have thought of the Aspen residents, with their wealth and support for the arts, as their own kind, with all the attendant understanding, while they paid lip service to the concerns of the residents along the Arkansas River.

ROAR's lawsuit is based on technical issues, but the underlying emotion is one of frustration, the inchoate rage of being rendered invisible. It is evident from their public statements that Christo and Jeanne-Claude chose the site for its aesthetic qualities and saw the land as an empty space for their taking. They refused to see the wider ramifications of *Over the River*, instead insisting that because they plan to remove all the anchors and cables, they were returning the land to its original state, ignoring the potential effects of the three years of drilling or removal, and narrowing their consideration of the impact on the community to the two-week viewing period. The environmental impact statements and the local concerns are at best inconveniences to be overcome, small-minded obstacles in the way of their benevolent genius.

Land art is not inherently problematic, but there will always be conflict, for public spaces have a multiplicity of meanings in which people with different interests are invested. It is not sufficient to assess these works solely based on their aesthetic qualities. Once an artist chooses to move out of the museum and gallery system, they are entering spaces with their own politics. The questions then are, is the artist creating a work that is in dialogue with these meanings, or are they just parachuting in without regard for the existing communities? Does the artist position themselves as more credible than the locals? Does the work engage with the relationships of the place or does it isolate itself from its context?

To put it another way, every place is somebody's home, and the question of home cannot be litigated. Whichever way the courts ultimately decide, *Over the River* raises an exigent question: What transgressions should we permit in the name of art?

Postscript: In January 2017, Christo announced that he would abandon *Over the River* as a protest against the Trump Administration, saying that the BLM is a federal agency and that he could not "do a project that benefits this landlord." Christo passed away in May 2020, at the age of eighty-four.

Flowers of Prison:
Ai Weiwei on Alcatraz

THE CHINESE ARTIST and activist Ai Weiwei smashed Han dynasty urns to make a statement on historical erasure and amnesia. He photographed his middle finger in front of, among other places, the Eiffel Tower, the White House, and Tiananmen Square. He photographed his wife lifting her skirt before Tiananmen Square. In 2011, he was arrested by Chinese authorities and held in solitary confinement for eighty-one days. He draws on this experience in a site-specific art installation that opened in September 2014: *@Large: Ai Weiwei on Alcatraz*.

In May 2008, after a massive earthquake hit the Sichuan province in west-central China, Ai led a citizen's investigation into the school collapses that killed thousands of children. Officials had told him the death toll was a secret. To learn the truth, Ai recruited volunteers via social media to visit the towns and interview the parents. On the first anniversary of the quake, he posted a list of 5,212 names of student casualties on his blog. This memorial doubled as an indictment of the government—because of graft, the schools had been shoddily built—and began Ai's troubles with Chinese authorities.

Ai made his name in the art world when he served as a design consultant for the 2008 Beijing Olympics "Bird's Nest" stadium. Another artist might have parlayed this fame into a lucrative career selling respectable artworks. Ai, however, sees the role of the artist in society as that of an activist. In particular, he advocates for freedom of expression and the individual conscience, which are the foundations of civil society. The day before the Beijing Olympics, he announced he would boycott the event and argued that the games had become a glittering cover for an autocratic regime. This boycott was similar to his work in Sichuan: it held those in power accountable to the people.

This unwavering belief in freedom and conscience stems from Ai's childhood in exile. Son of poet Ai Qing, he was a year old in 1958 when his father was sentenced to hard labor for criticizing Mao Zedong and the Communist Party. The year before, Mao had encouraged citizens to openly air their views of the regime, only to turn around and crack down on dissident intellectuals. The younger Ai grew up watching his father scrub latrines and threaten to kill himself. He could not go to school. One winter in the frozen deserts of northwest China, the family lived in a dugout and scavenged for food. They returned to Beijing only after Mao died in 1976.

After Ai posted the list of student names online, authorities shut down his blog and put him under surveillance. In August 2009, he went to Chengdu, Sichuan's provincial capital, to testify at the trial of Tan Zuoren, another earthquake activist who had been accused of "incitement to subversion of state power." Like Ai, Tan had been investigating the school collapses and collecting the names of the victims. At three in the morning, police knocked on Ai's door on the pretext of checking identity papers. They beat him up and detained him for twelve hours, causing him to miss the trial. Tan was sentenced to five years in prison.

That September, Ai went to Munich to prepare for his exhibition *So Sorry* at the Haus der Kunst. As part of the show, he used 9,000 backpacks in five colors to write on the museum façade in Chinese, "For seven years she lived happily on this earth," quoting the mother of one of the Sichuan earthquake victims. When Ai arrived in Munich, he complained that the intermittent headaches he had been having for a month had become unbearable. Doctors found a hemorrhage in his brain, likely from the blows from the Chengdu police, and he successfully underwent emergency surgery.

Before the 2008 Olympics, Shanghai invited Ai to build a new studio in their arts district. In November 2010, the city deemed the building illegal and ordered it demolished. Ai knew that this was retaliation for his activism, and in protest, he held a party, inviting his supporters to feast on 10,000 river crabs. In the Chinese language, the phrase for "river crab," *he xie,* is homonymous to "harmonious," which the government uses in its slogan "The realization of a harmonious society." To many Chinese online denizens, this saying is used to justify the repression of dissent, and *he xie* has become slang for censorship. On the day of the event, authorities put Ai under house arrest without explanation, and the fete went on without him. The studio was destroyed in January 2011.

That April, Ai was about to catch a flight to Hong Kong when he was arrested at the Beijing airport. He was held at an undisclosed location for eighty-one days and disallowed contact with his family. The government charged him with tax evasion and released him on the condition that he did not give interviews, stayed away from social media, and could not leave Beijing. Within months, he was back on Twitter and speaking to the press. He can now travel outside the capital, but the government has not returned his passport.

Alcatraz hardly needs an introduction. It is America's most notorious penitentiary. Between 1934 and 1963, it housed some of the nation's worst criminals, including the mob boss Al Capone and the "Birdman" Robert Stroud. Many of the inmates were transferred there after they caused trouble at other prisons. The cells were primitive, guards stripped and beat inmates, and in the early years, the prisoners could not talk to one another, even at mealtimes. Its location adds to its mystique; perched on a rock outcrop in the cold, brutal currents of the San Francisco Bay, Alcatraz is within reach of the city and yet so far away.

Most of us know Alcatraz as the inescapable fortress we see in books and movies. But it has other, lesser-known histories. The Spanish named it for the multitude of seabirds that nest on the island. It was a military fort during the Civil War, part of the coastal defense against the Confederacy. Later, it held prisoners of conscience, including Hopi men who refused to send their children to boarding schools and conscientious objectors from World War I. And beginning in 1969, Native American activists occupied the island for nineteen months to protest federal Indian policies. It is now a major tourist attraction, drawing an average of 4,000 visitors a day.

The idea to stage an art exhibition on Alcatraz began with Cheryl Haines, executive director of the For-Site Foundation, a San Francisco organization dedicated to art about place. For her, cities are also settings to showcase art. She was opening a show in the Presidio when she saw the lights of Alcatraz and wanted to work there, though she did not yet have an artist in mind. In 2011, she visited Ai after his release from detention and asked what she could do to help. He wanted to bring his art to a larger audience, and she said, "What if I bring you a prison?"

Ai describes himself as a "remote control artist." Even before his passport was revoked, he often came up with ideas and has a team of artisans and assistants to execute the work. Because he cannot leave China, he could not visit Alcatraz and see the place for himself. Instead, Haines flew to Beijing to sneak him photographs, videos, and architectural drawings of the island. From his Beijing compound, he conceived seven site-specific pieces for Alcatraz, choosing materials that would not look suspicious to Chinese customs officers. The parts were then flown to San Francisco and ferried to Alcatraz, where handlers reassembled them as Ai supervised by videoconference.

I happened to be in San Francisco and went to see *@Large*. It was Fleet Week and the Blue Angels, the Navy's flight demonstration squad, practiced their acrobatics over the blue bay waters. In the distance, fog gathered on the summit of Angel Island, the lesser-known prison island on the bay; from 1910 to 1940, it detained Chinese immigrants under the 1882 Chinese Exclusion Act. I had been to Alcatraz a few years ago and thought the salt breeze, the cormorants in flight, and the views of the city and the bay must have intensified the prisoners' isolation. The landscape heightened the cruelty of Alcatraz.

A colorful dragon greeted visitors at the New Industries Building, the former factory where inmates with privileges could work. Its eyes bulge with birds that resemble the Twitter logo. Instead of a traditional dragon train in red or yellow—which represent prosperity and royalty respectively—its body is made of kites hung from the ceiling and decorated with birds and flowers. A number of kites carry quotes from exiles and political prisoners, beginning with Edward Snowden's "Privacy is a function of liberty" and ending with Ai himself: "Every one of us is a potential convict." More kite sculptures of birds and flowers hover at the corners of the dilapidated room.

I laughed when I saw the dragon. In Chinese culture, the dragon is revered as a symbol of power and imperial rule. The dragon dance is often performed on Chinese New Year to bring luck and fortune. In *With Wind,* Ai transforms this motif of tradition and authority into a celebration of self-expression. The birds and flowers imbue the creature with the beauty of the natural world. They also reflect Alcatraz's landscape: outside the prison walls, seagulls nest on the rocky shores. In spring, gardens of roses, honeysuckles, irises, and many more I cannot identify come into bloom; during the penitentiary years, prisoners could work in the gardens and find respite in nature. *With Wind* makes a direct political statement, but Ai livens the work with a sense of play. This dragon may be trapped in a prison, but it lets our thoughts fly.

In the next room, Ai covers the floor with 176 Lego portraits of prisoners of conscience from around the world. Some of them are well known in the English-speaking world, such as Nelson Mandela, Martin Luther King Jr., and Chelsea Manning. Most of the people Ai profiled do not make the international news. The United States is not beyond his critique: Ai includes six people from this country. A number are from Vietnam, Iran, and Bahrain. He includes thirty-eight prisoners from China, the highest of any nation represented, from Uighur and Tibetan independence activists to the writer and Nobel laureate Liu Xiaobo. Along a wall, binders tell the stories of each of these people. This text is also accessible on the exhibition website.

I have to admit, I tried to remember these stories, but I only got as far as three or four names before my eyes started to glaze over. And as I begin writing this essay two weeks later, I cannot remember what I read. The volume of information that *Trace* presents is overwhelming. It highlights the conditions of political imprisonment, but if it is meant to educate, the average viewer is unlikely to remember the stories. It reminds governments that someone is watching, but it is unlikely to change their minds; authoritarian power is often convinced that it is right. The power of *Trace* lies in its insistence on witness: it seeks to record and remember what we are told to forget. It holds *us* accountable: it is when we forget that power can run amok.

Refraction, the last of the sculptures at New Industries, looks like a giant metallic bird on the verge of flight. It can be seen only from the gun gallery, a narrow corridor from which armed guards watched over prisoners at work. This vantage point situates the viewer in a position of power, able only to look down from afar and never intimately. The wings of this strange creature hold Tibetan solar cookers, a fact I gleaned only from the docent on duty. I suppose if it were not caged in this prison factory, it might fly like the seagulls outside. But as I looked at it through the broken windows, I thought it was not meant to move.

The other four installations are located in the Cellhouse, the main prison block at the top of a steep hill. In twelve of the cells of the A Block, Ai pipes in speeches, poems, and songs by artists and activists who have been persecuted for their words. Each work can be heard only from inside its tiny cell, where Ai provides silver stools for visitors to sit and listen. In one cell, Martin Luther King Jr. delivers "Beyond Vietnam," a speech in which he linked racism and segregation to capitalist war machinery. In another, the Russian punk collective Pussy Riot shrieks "Virgin Mary, Put Putin Away," originally performed at a Moscow Orthodox church and for which three members were jailed. In yet another cell, Tibetan singer Lolo serenades "Raise the Tibetan Flag."

I did not know most of the languages Ai featured in *Stay Tuned.* I did not need to. I felt the passion, despair, and urgency in the rhythms and modulations of these voices. Some of the songs tell stories. Others are calls to action. Yet others are lyrical evocations of life in prison. The original texts and translations are provided on boards outside each of the cells; they are also available, together with the recordings, on the exhibition website. The voices seemed to demand we slow down and pay attention to the lyrics, the story each tune seeks to tell, but I was too antsy to sit still. I wandered in and out of the cells, sampling moments from each song, creating a sort of mixtape of my own. Taken together, these disembodied voices haunt the prison with their defiance.

Ai uses piped voices again in *Illumination,* this time Tibetan and Hopi chants in twin psychiatric observation rooms at the Alcatraz Hospital, a full-service medical facility adjacent to the cellblocks. These two "bug rooms" are more claustrophobic than the regular cells. The thick glass panes allow in little light. The doors are solid with small windows, presumably for guards to check in on their wards. Compared to the peeling paint, shattered glass, and crumbling walls of much of the island, these two rooms are well preserved, as if a place apart from the prison block. They are also at the heart of Alcatraz, away from the wind and salt off the bay, perhaps a metaphor for the intimate self we strive to protect against assault.

In this brutal prison, a number of inmates snapped—the official estimate is 2 percent, though it is likely higher—and were confined to the psychiatric ward. Al Capone, who suffered from syphilitic dementia, spent most of his sentence at the hospital. Ai was put in solitary for most of his detention and watched by two guards all the time, an environment designed to break down his psychological defenses. Both the Tibetans and Hopis are people subjugated for their differences and persecuted for insisting on their cultures. I thought of all this as I listened to the incantations. I thought of Ai Qing, suicidal in the deserts of Xinjiang. We think of chanting as meditation and celebration, but here its rituals also become a stay against insanity.

In *Blossom*, Ai fills some of the sinks, toilets, and bathtubs of the hospital wards with white ceramic flowers. Their fragile beauty stands out amid the ruins of the prison. They are also likely a comment on the Hundred Flowers Campaign, that period Mao Zedong opened the Communist Party to criticism and later cracked down on dissidents. The multitude of flowers is signature Ai, reminiscent of the 10,000 river crabs and 9,000 backpacks, as well as the millions of handcrafted sunflower seeds he scattered on the floor of the Tate in 2010. For Ai, large numbers of handmade objects represent beautiful societies of individuals. In these white flowers, I also saw an offering: to the sick, the imprisoned, and the potential convict in each of us.

In the dining hall, directly below the hospital, Ai invites visitors to send postcards to the prisoners profiled in *Trace*. For him, the hardest part of prison was the isolation, the sense that the world outside had forgotten him. In *Yours Truly*, the handwritten notes would give the prisoners some human contact and ultimately hope. The postcards are pre-addressed and each decorated with a bird or flower native to the prisoner's country. They are arranged, image side up, on two shelves. The binders of profiles are set on benches for visitors to browse. Between the shelves are bins for visitors to drop off postcards.

The postcards are a good idea in theory, but I wondered if they would reach their intended recipients, for prison guards would likely intercept them. Looked at this way, *Yours Truly* is an exercise in futility. And I have to admit too, I did not write a postcard. I thought about it and even held one in my hand—I think it was to Ethiopia—but I did not know what to say, what I had to say. I watched people look up the binders and scribble notes to people they would likely never meet. I wondered what they wrote. I wondered what they thought as they wrote. Did they think they were making change? Maybe these postcards are meant for us to pause and reflect.

For Ai Weiwei, art is politics and "an artist must also be an activist." He aims to effect change through his work. On one hand, this sentiment seems naïve; the likelihood that *@Large* would play a role in the release of political prisoners is close to none. The installations, while individually powerful, ultimately make perfunctory gestures toward Alcatraz and its sense of place, likely because Ai could not experience the island for himself. But Ai strikes authoritarian power at its most vulnerable spot: its sense of legitimacy and moral authority. He opens conversations on the nature of power and the possibilities of art. And *@Large* is a giant finger to the forces trying to silence him: he refuses to be cowed.

Postscript: Chinese authorities returned Ai's passport in July 2015. He moved to Berlin and now lives in Cambridge, United Kingdom.

Split

ON MARCH 11, 2011, the day an earthquake and tsunami damaged the Fukushima Daiichi nuclear power plant on Japan's Honshu Island, I saw Allison Smith's mixed-media installation *Piece Work* at the Museum of Contemporary Art Denver. At the center of the exhibit was a collection of Smith's handmade renditions of cloth gas masks used during the First World War. Her intimate needlework suggested the domesticity of war, of women allaying their fears and anxieties through the repetition of sewing and knitting for the men on the battlefront. Gas masks protect their wearers from the invisible poisons in the atmosphere, but they also conceal identities and turn soldiers into contingents of anonymous bodies. As I looked at the rows of hollowed eyes inside a glass case, I thought that these cloth masks would be ineffective against chlorine gas—as well as in a nuclear disaster.

All that morning, I followed the news reports out of Japan. The reactors had shut down immediately when the quake occurred, but the tsunami crossed a seawall, flooded the backup generators, and left the plant without power to run its cooling systems. The fuel rods began to overheat. The heat evaporated the water in the cooling pools and exposed the rods. The pressure in the reactors built up. The day after the quake, an explosion tore off the roof and outer walls of Unit 1. Two days later, an explosion in Unit 3 damaged its exterior walls. The Tokyo

Electric Power Company, the plant operator, initially tried to reassure the public that Unit 2 was stable, but four days after the quake, it suffered a blast that warranted a temporary evacuation of the plant. In an attempt to keep the fuel rods submerged in water, Japan began pumping seawater into the reactors, the nuclear equivalent of a Hail Mary.

Half a world away from the disaster, I went about my life as usual. I went to work. I visited the art museum. I rode my bike around the prairie near my home. I made dinner. I did not rush out to buy potassium iodide pills, as many Americans did, but I felt a heightened alertness and a sense of vulnerability. The fabric of everyday life had ruptured, the routines of thought disrupted. I had a sense that a wall had crumbled and I had turned permeable. I was immersed in the present, but I also felt another kind of receptivity: I knew that if I were in the path of the fallout, I would be subject to its dangers. My body would absorb the radioactive iodine and potassium in the air. The poisons would lodge in my bones, my thyroid, and over the decades emit elevated levels of radiation and scramble the codes in my cells.

Smith cites German philosopher Peter Sloterdijk's critical essay *Terror from the Air* as a touchstone for her art. Sloterdijk argues that the modern era began on April 22, 1915, when the German army attacked French troops at Ypres with chlorine gas. This first act of gas warfare killed the enemy by making the atmospheric conditions untenable for life, a departure from traditional warfare in which soldiers impart direct blows onto the enemy's body. "By using violence against the very air that groups breathe," Sloterdijk writes, "the human being's immediate atmospheric envelope is transformed into something whose intactness or non-intactness is henceforth a question." That is to say, we can no longer take our atmosphere, the very air we breathe to live, for granted—like in a nuclear disaster.

The modern condition, Sloterdijk argues, is characterized by anxiety about our environment. Gas warfare, he writes, "is about integrating the most fundamental strata of the biological conditions for life into the attack: the breather, by continuing his elementary habitus, i.e., the necessity to breathe, becomes at once a victim and an unwilling accomplice in his own annihilation." In the Second World War, we saw this again in Auschwitz, where thousands of Jews were gassed; in the bombings of Dresden, where the intense heat cooked the flesh of those who hid in bomb shelters; and in the bombings of Hiroshima and Nagasaki, where the radioactive fallout lodged in the bodies of those who did not perish immediately. After the war, we sprayed chemicals on our crops and rangelands from the air.

Smith's gas masks explicate this sense of danger. In the exhibition catalog, she says of the originals she saw at Les Invalides in Paris, a military museum, "To me, they seemed somehow lovingly made, and functionally inadequate. I was stuck with the recurring thought, 'someone made this', and I tried to imagine what that would be like." In *Piece Work,* she reenacts this act of making, reminding us of the role of craft in war. She also brings our latent anxiety about our environment into focus. And the masks are blank slates. We wear them to assuage our fears, but in doing so, we cover our faces and erase our individualities, our sense of self.

In the first days of Fukushima, the media reported that the crisis was not as severe as the 1979 partial nuclear meltdown at Pennsylvania's Three Mile Island reactor. Then it likely surpassed Three Mile Island. And it could always turn into the next Chernobyl. Hiroshima and Nagasaki were also invoked. The media relied on public memory of these linchpins of nuclear disasters to contend with the chaos in Fukushima. Despite all the efforts to whitewash the dangers of nuclear power, we still remember its catastrophic potential. Japan is the only country to have been attacked by nuclear bombs as weapons of war, yet their contemporary science textbooks make no mention of the downsides of nuclear power. Fukushima reopened this rupture and revisited the nightmare of the bombs: blistered skins, charred bodies, a metallic taste in the mouth, high rates of cancer, and children born with deformities.

As I watched helicopters drop water on the smoking reactors, I kept thinking of Chernobyl, which I had lived through as a toddler in London. I don't remember the event directly, but my parents often tell the story of how they tried to find powdered milk on the supermarket shelves for my sister and me. London was at the tail end of the fallout, but Britain imports food from continental Europe, which was directly in the path of the prevailing winds. I also thought of Hiroshima and Nagasaki. I grew up in Singapore, where the history textbooks and evening television dramas tell of the terror and brutality of the Japanese occupation. For my forebears, for my grandparents, the atomic bombs meant liberation from bowing to Japanese soldiers under the threat of beatings, massacres of Chinese men on the beaches, and an inadequate diet of sweet potatoes and yam.

The day before the earthquake, the United States Nuclear Regulatory Commission renewed Vermont Yankee's license for another twenty years despite tritium leaks and the collapse of a cooling tower. The Vermont Senate had earlier voted against this extension. The design of Vermont Yankee is virtually identical to that of the troubled reactors in Fukushima and it was not built to run for another two decades. Two weeks after the quake, I heard *The Guardian* reporter George Monbiot argue on *Democracy Now* that coal is a far more dangerous technology than nuclear power. He said that coal kills two thousand people a week in China, a far greater death toll than that from Chernobyl for twenty-five years. His tally from Chernobyl: forty-three. *The Onion* perhaps said it best, one week after the earthquake: "Nuclear Energy Advocates Insist US Reactors Completely Safe Unless Something Bad Happens."

On the International Nuclear Event Scale, which assesses the severity of a nuclear accident, Three Mile Island ranks at five, an "accident with offsite risk," and Chernobyl at seven, a "major accident" and the highest reading on the scale. With explosions in four reactors, uncovered spent fuel pools, likely meltdowns in three cores, damaged cooling systems, erratic surges in radiation levels, and workers pumping seawater into the units with fire hoses, Japan initially rated the event at four, an "accident without significant off-site risk." A week later, they raised it to five. Only a month later did they raise it to seven while reiterating that the fallout was still less than that of Chernobyl. Around the same time, robots entered Units 1 and 3 to measure the temperatures, pressures, and radiation levels. It was still too dangerous for humans to begin repairs.

The invisibility of the radioactive fallout meant that we could not trust our senses to assess the dangers in the atmosphere and were instead dependent on the authorities. And in the initial days of the disaster, the official assessments varied wildly. The readings of the radiation levels fluctuated from next to nothing at the gate of the plant to levels high enough to warrant temporary evacuations. One day, Tokyo warned that the levels of radioactive iodine in its water supply had exceeded the recommended limit for infants, though still safe for adults; the next day, the water was all good again. The Japanese government evacuated a zone of twelve miles around the plant, while America recommended that its citizens living within fifty miles of the plant head south or leave the country altogether. At least chlorine gas has a distinctive smell and color.

The Japanese government also recommended that the people who lived between twelve and nineteen miles from the distressed plant stay indoors. The walls may serve as barricades of sorts against the poisons in the atmosphere, but no house is completely sealed off from the outside. Spaces need to be ventilated, air circulated. Perhaps some protection is better than none at all, but the authorities also reflexively saw the indoors as a zone of safety. In the face of danger, they ordered people into hiding, into isolation, and into fear, the psychological equivalent of wearing a cloth gas mask. The home was no longer a place of rest and refuge; it became instead a fortress to keep ourselves apart. I saw the implicit message, one that we already take for granted in our destabilizing environment: Be suspicious of the unknown. Split yourself from the world.

Footsteps on the Sea

A DECADE AGO, I bought Rebecca Solnit's essay collection *Storming the Gates of Paradise: Landscapes for Politics* on a lark.

At that time, I was beginning to write, trying to find my voice. Three years before that, I had moved to Colorado with the boy I would eventually marry. I took a gamble then; I did not know what the future would bring, but I had an inkling that it would be in the American West. We moved to arid Colorado at the height of summer, when the prairie around Denver had already turned brown. But when we drove up the Rockies, along rivers that carved out deep canyons and peaks that dissolved into the sky, I knew this was where I needed to be.

One of my earliest attempts to write was of the San Rafael Swell in Utah, on a road trip to Los Angeles. We had assumed that Utah and Nevada would be empty and planned to speed through them. Instead, we found ourselves in the red lands where canyons scallop to the horizon and rocks twist into arches. The land is stark and arid, dotted with tiny shrubs and the occasional juniper. I tried to write about the openness of this land, the clarity of the light, and the sense of disorientation. I had no idea how to say what I wanted to say, but it was in these efforts that I began to write. I continued trying to write about the western landscapes, but I kept finding myself at the gates of Nature. Nature, as I knew then, was a paradise to be fenced off from the ugliness of the world.

I had seen Solnit's byline in magazines such as *Orion* and *The Nation*. Her range of subjects, unorthodox conclusions, and gorgeous language had all wowed me. In an *Orion* piece published before the Beijing Olympic Games, she writes not about China's human rights abuses or intrepid celebrations of sports, but that the sleek beauty of athletes' bodies is "co-opted by a culture that wants to be seen as natural, legitimate, stirring, beautiful." Nations use their athletes' bodies as masks to cover up abuses of power elsewhere. These themes of the politics of nature and the body had begun to surface in my work, so when I saw *Storming the Gates of Paradise* on the shelves of the Boulder Bookstore, I picked it up without hesitation.

"It was a place that taught me to write," Solnit says in the introduction. In the late 1980s, she had gone to the antinuclear demonstrations at the Nevada Test Site. There she camped in a spectacular desert, made friends with artists and visionaries, and played tag with authorities, an experience that led her to make the connections between nature, politics, history, and memory. In her second book *Savage Dreams*, another of my favorites, she writes of her experiences in a polyphony of voices we often think of as disparate, as a journalist, an art and cultural critic, and a memoirist. She weaves these voices into a compelling portrait of a place we think of as desolate and investigates how our stories of this place reflect who we are.

In *Storming the Gates of Paradise,* Solnit writes of the Nevada desert and the histories of San Francisco, where she has lived for most of her adult life. She wonders what our stories about the sky and about America's heavily militarized border with Mexico have to say about us; she explores the impacts of mining and of the constraints on women's freedom to roam. She writes about storm clouds gathering above the New Mexico prairie, promising rain that never seems to arrive, and the existential wastelands of suburban Los Angeles. "Paradise," she writes, "is a Persian word that originally meant an enclosed garden." In these essays, she explicates the ways we fence off our gardens and seeks ways to tear these fences down.

The first essay "The Red Lands" is set in the Nevada desert. I have read it a dozen times, and I still find surprises. She begins at Lee Vining, in the rain shadow of the Sierra Nevada, where she overhears a man on a payphone trying to make amends with his wife. From here she segues into desert ecology, the scale of the landscape, the effects of nuclear testing, the ongoing wars in faraway deserts, the cowboy mythos, and the seductiveness of it all. "The evils in this country tend to generate their opposites," she writes. "And the landscape of the West seems like the stage on which such dramas are played out, a space without boundaries, in which anything can be realized, a moral ground, out here where your shadow can stretch hundreds of feet just before sunset, where you loom large, and lonely."

In the weeks after I read these essays, I walked around disoriented, as though the ground under my feet had turned to quicksand. I felt that I had been gifted with lenses with which I could begin to see below the surfaces of things. The trees and rivers and grasslands, the roads and buildings and alleys of my everyday life became rich with meanings and associations. I tried to respond, to engage with Solnit. In these scribblings, my voice and opinions were tentative, but I began to understand my beliefs and find the subjects about which I wanted to write.

With the benefit of hindsight, I see that the central question I was trying to ask was, how do we access truth? What do we know and how do we come to know it? What don't we see and what are the ramifications of this invisibility? When I started writing, I kept looking over my shoulder, as if there were a specter watching me, ready to punish if I stepped out of line. I rarely write from my life—it is not in my temperament—but maybe the act of writing itself is the betrayal. Writing, after all, is a lot about wrestling with the messes of life on the page, taking what we are taught to keep inside and giving voice to it, even if it only goes into a drawer at first. I am more compelled to engage with public issues, but this compulsion is driven by the questions I confront in my private life.

I was flailing. Solnit's peripatetic style of putting seemingly disparate subjects in conversation with each other, of provoking questions more than giving answers, showed me a way to challenge our worn assumptions and approach truths hidden in plain sight. And she showed me how writing is a practice with which we can learn to give testimony and develop credibility.

My breakthrough came when I visited Alcatraz the following spring. On that trip I had wanted to go to Angel Island, to see the poems that the Chinese detainees wrote on the barrack walls, but my friends and I missed the only ferry from Fisherman's Wharf that morning and bought tickets for the other prison island on the bay instead.

Alcatraz is a rock outcrop infamous for the penitentiary it housed from 1934 to 1963. It was meant to be the prison of last resort as well as for the most violent and high-profile criminals of the time. Al Capone, who was brought down on charges of tax evasion, was one of the first inmates on the island. The "Birdman" Robert Stroud, nicknamed for his obsession with birds, was transferred to solitary confinement on Alcatraz after he stabbed an orderly at McNeil Island and killed a guard at Leavenworth. Alcatraz was known for its high security, but geography provided the ultimate fence: it was believed that no one could cross the San Francisco Bay alive.

Maybe it is the force of the San Joaquin and Sacramento Rivers flowing into the Pacific. Maybe it is our lurid fascination with law and order, violence and control. But Alcatraz continues to captivate our fickle imagination. In 1962, Frank Morris, John Anglin, and Clarence Anglin chiseled a hole in the walls with spoons for over a year. They left dummies fashioned from papier-mâché and climbed an air vent. The figures fooled the guards and bought them a few hours to scale the fences and build a makeshift raft out of stolen raincoats. The next day, police found the remains of the raft on Angel Island. It is widely believed that the men drowned in the Bay, but whether they had made it to shore is still the subject of speculation.

That day, I began to make connections between landscape and belief. It would be another four months before I would visit Angel Island for the first time and another few years before I understood that it would be a touchstone for my writing. But on Alcatraz, I began to see how I could interpret a place for myself, to move beyond the popular narratives for a more complex truth. And, despite the different itinerary, I still had the Angel Island poems in mind. I was in the middle of my immigration journey, one fraught with the possibility that no matter how hard I worked and adhered to the rules, my visa could be denied solely based on a lottery or quota, forces outside of my control. On Alcatraz, I began to see how the landscape shaped the detention center on Angel Island.

Some notes from Alcatraz:

The uniform rows of windows reflect the homogeneity of prison life, the inmates stripped of their identities and turned into numbers. Alcatraz was designed to be a fortress, with an aura of hard edges, a place beyond forgiveness and redemption. But the walls are also crumbling, the ruin quickened by wind and salt off the bay, and I imagined the island shrouded in sepia, the memory of violence abandoned to nature. We walked on a broken concrete path lined with pink and yellow flowers. They gave off a sweet scent that wafted in the breeze.

Alcatraz, I thought, could be a garden. Then I stepped inside the prison.

Inside the prison, the air was still. I knew I was just a visitor, free to come and go as I wished, but I felt as if I had been cut off from the world outside. The walls were a hard grey and the windows shut out the breeze. Rows of disused showerheads lined up on overhead bars. I imagined the ghosts of inmates past, watching one another with wary eyes, without privacy even in this most intimate of routines.

I shuddered.

The cells are stacked three stories high. None are next to an exterior wall. Most measure nine by five feet. Each cell contains a bed, a small desk, a sink, and a toilet. In solitary, the doors are solid with a tiny window. In the regular cells, the opening is barricaded with metal grates. There are four cell blocks, A through D. At the end of each block is a gun gallery from which armed guards kept the prisoners under surveillance. As we walked around the cells, a park ranger—Alcatraz is now under the purview of the National Park Service—rolled the metal grates open and shut, ostensibly to simulate the cacophony of prison life. Steel clashed on steel, and the walls amplified the noise.

I wanted to escape. I reached for the door to the recreational yard. Outside, the sun was a blast of light and relief. Here prisoners with privileges could play sports on the weekends. For many, it was their only opportunity to socialize and exercise. I stood at the top of the stairs and looked beyond the barbed wire to San Francisco. The skyscrapers and hills and Victorian homes with vast bay windows appeared as if they had risen from the sea toward the sky. From Alcatraz, the city looked like freedom. But I was leaving later in the day. For the prisoners whose sentences seemed infinite, this view might have intensified their isolation, the city only an apparition in the fog.

Back at my desk, as I tried to parse the meanings of this place, I turned to *Storming the Gates of Paradise.* I knew what I had seen, but I did not yet know how I could convey it in a compelling way, how to blend facts and anecdotes with my subject position to create a work that is at once illuminating, rigorous, and sublime. I did not yet know how to integrate my thoughts and experience into something that resembled coherence. In Solnit's essays, I saw that research is not the sole province of the dull and rigid, but instead a living process with which we can interrogate the nature of truth and knowledge, construct new frameworks, and forge dialogues across subjects and disciplines.

Over the years, as I keep coming back to Solnit's book, I feel like I am returning home. I find nuances I have not noticed before. I find answers to questions I have been asking. I find new ways to ask the questions that matter most to me: about place, about identity, and about journeys. Many times I start writing a new piece in my head. In reading this book I began to build an encyclopedia of images and meanings, a foundation with which I could engage the world.

Here is an attempt:

At Alcatraz, geraniums and honeysuckles, irises and roses, white yarrow, and poppies bloom in the hillsides around the prison. The flowers are large and colorful, rivaling the best botanical gardens in the world. It is, in Solnit's terms, a paradise—literally an enclosed garden, a patch of beauty in a prison better known for its cruelties. Alcatraz was a fort during the Civil War and though the soil was rocky and barren, military families planted the first gardens, trying to make a home out of this place. In the penitentiary years, warden James Johnston allowed some inmates to work in these gardens. Where detainees on Angel Island turned to poetry, on Alcatraz inmates with privileges could tend to life and soil.

As Delphine Hirasuna, author of *Gardens of Alcatraz*, writes, these gardens are "testaments to the human spirit."

Elliott Michener was one of the inmates whose life changed in these gardens. Imprisoned for counterfeiting, he was transferred to Alcatraz after he attempted to escape from Leavenworth. When he returned a dropped key to a guard, he was given the privilege to work in the gardens. He built terraces, a toolshed, and even a greenhouse. He composted kitchen scraps. He was also authorized to order seed catalogs and choose the flowers and bulbs he wanted. After his release, he made a living as a landscaper. He said of this experience, "The hillsides provided a refuge from the disturbances of the prison, the work a release, and it became an obsession, the one thing I would do well."

This I wrote too, though it would take me longer to figure out what it meant:

In 1775, Spanish naval officer Juan de Ayala arrived in the San Francisco Bay and named Alcatraz for the multitude of seabirds he found on the island. I saw the birds everywhere too, perched on the ruins of the warden's house, floating on the surf, nestled in the grasses and gardens. They could fly. They could escape from Alcatraz. As I watched them I wanted to fly too, but I remembered that one of the Angel Island poems begins:

The seascape resembles lichen twisting and turning for a
    thousand *li*.
There is no shore to land and it is difficult to walk.

Letter to the Arctic

I DON'T KNOW YOU PERSONALLY, but a trip to visit you might contribute to your demise. I have been near though, in southeastern Alaska and Iceland, landscapes of perennial snow and ice tempered by warm ocean currents, but I have not crossed the Arctic Circle into the true land of the midnight sun. You are the far north, an inhospitable place of extremes, a place where our dreams meet fantasy. You loom large in our imaginations. I know there are people indigenous to your land, who know your ways inside out. But for most of us from less demanding climates, you push us to the limits of our endurance and knowledge.

Perhaps this is why we venerate and denigrate you at the same time. There may be plenty of pictures of you in books, magazines, and videos, but looking at images is not the same as being there, immersed in the textures of your lichen, glaciers, and aurora borealis. On some level, I feel that even if I get to visit you someday, you will remain unknowable. I don't know what they are, obviously, but I know you have your secrets that you would only reveal gradually, if even that much and if we made the space to listen to you. I respect that. I respect that you don't want to give away everything at once, keeping your soul for only those who care about you enough.

There are people who see the oil beneath your ice sheets as resources to be exploited. They want to destroy the delicate balance of life you have sustained for thousands of years to get at the riches. It is easy to say they are greedy, that profits matter to them above everything else, but I think their malice drills deeper than that. They are afraid of your wildness. You exist outside of their imagination and experience. They know they cannot survive your harsh conditions. They see your unknowability as a dark hole, an uncanny shadow they cannot begin to comprehend. They want to tame you, shrink you into something they can control.

I say they, but in some ways, I am also a part of them. I understand the need to preserve wild places, to keep ecological and human communities intact, but I also like to drive and travel and keep my thermostat between seventy and seventy-five degrees year-round. I try to reduce my footprint, but ultimately, I come from diasporic people who have uprooted themselves over and over again. I don't have an ancestral land to call home. I don't have a refuge from the vagaries of the world. The only system I have known is capitalism. As much as I try to counter its excesses, it is also the system by which I get my food and shelter.

Our desire to tear up your land for its resources is not the only thing harming you. Your sea ice has been melting, so much so that you will likely be free of summer sea ice sooner rather than later. Your permafrost is thawing and releasing the trapped methane into the atmosphere. In June 2020, you hit a record surface temperature of over one hundred degrees Fahrenheit. The Northwest Passage has been completely open in the last few summers. These wounds impact everything from the ability of polar bears to find food to the growth of lichen in the tundra. And in the larger scheme of things, all that melting ice is raising the sea level and devastating coastal communities far from you.

I wish I could say I am doing all that I can to help you. But I admit that I often feel powerless, that the little things I do are not enough. And I live in a system where I must create "value," even if it is destructive, to pay rent. I can critique our warped notions that equate value with capital, but I have not figured out how to step away from it all and still survive. But this much I know: the change we need to make is larger than any one person. I don't want to say that it would be too late to save you, for I know you have an intelligence more creative and a spirit more resilient than ours. But I hope that if I get to meet you someday, you will not have irrevocably changed.

IV

Apocalypses

Borders and Citizens

ON AUGUST 12, 2015, almost twelve years from the day I first arrived in America, I was sworn in as a US citizen.

My journey to the Promised Land—which hinged on education, work, and marriage—was easier than most but not without anxiety. In 2006, I graduated from the University of Michigan and found a job in Denver. My employment and authorization to stay in America was contingent on receiving a professional work visa, the H1-B. In 2004, despite the strong economy, President George W. Bush had reduced the cap on H1-B visas from 195,000 to 65,000 a year. The year I applied, there were three times as many applicants as available visas, and USCIS held a lottery to determine which applications they would review.

I did not win the lottery that year, but as a citizen of Singapore, I was eligible for the H1-B1, a special class of visas created under the Singapore-United States Free Trade Agreement. The catch was that I could not apply for permanent residency while I held the H1-B1. My then-boyfriend, now-husband had a green card then, which meant he could sponsor me if we married, but there were also quotas for spouses of permanent residents, and I would have to wait months or even a year or two for a green card, during which time I would likely have to leave the country. If I had wanted to get married and have children then, I risked separation from my family.

I was on the H1-B1 for two years before I finally hit the H1-B jackpot. These were also the years of the Great Recession. The H1 visas must be sponsored by an employer—if you lose your job at any point, you lose your visa status. I'm not sure what I would have done if I had lost my job; I was lucky that I worked for a fiscally prudent company.

My husband proposed to me on the day of his citizenship test. I joked, "Did you pass?" As the spouse of a US citizen, I was no longer subject to a quota, and I received my green card within three months of application. The green card is conditional: after two years, I had to prove to immigration officials that I was still happily married. Luckily for me, I did not marry an abuser. A friend's well-intentioned marriage to a US citizen fell apart in less than two years, and he spent a great deal on attorney fees to resolve his green card issues, worrying for months that he would not be allowed to continue the life he had built here.

As the spouse of a US citizen, I could apply for citizenship within three years of receiving my green card, which I did. At this point, my citizenship grants me the inalienable right to live in this country. It also affirms that I am a part of the body politic.

I wrote a version of this essay in the early months of 2016 when Donald Trump was a candidate whose nativist rhetoric propelled him to the front of the Republican primaries. He said, among other things, that Mexican immigrants are rapists, that he would deport all undocumented immigrants, that he would rescind birthright citizenship, and that he would build a wall on our southern border and make Mexico pay for it. He also equated Muslims with "radical Islamic terrorists" and called for an entry ban on all Muslims, including refugees. While he vacillated on some of the details, the overall message was clear: He wanted to restrict immigration on the basis of race and religion.

Weeks after Trump's inauguration, he has already issued an executive order, "Protecting the Nation from Foreign Terrorist Entry into the United States," which suspends entry from seven Muslim-majority countries for 90 days, suspends the refugee admission program for 120 days, and bars Syrian refugees for the indefinite future. The order was effective immediately, which meant that a number of people were already in the air when their entry status changed.

Chaos ensued at airports as immigration officials tried to figure out who was admissible and who was not. Many people with valid visas to enter the United States were detained for hours. Some were deported. Two Iraqi men detained at New York's John F. Kennedy International Airport—a translator for US troops during the Iraq War and a man on his way to join his wife and seven-year-old son in Houston—became plaintiffs in a lawsuit filed by the American Civil Liberties Union (ACLU). In an emergency hearing in a Brooklyn court, a judge issued a stay on portions of the order. The ACLU has also won stays in three other courts, but they mostly cover people who were already in the air when the order came down.

The executive order maximized suffering on the basis of race and religion.

Exclusion laws are not new to America. In 1882, Congress passed the Chinese Exclusion Act, and in 1889, the US Supreme Court upheld its legality on the grounds of national security. The law banned the entry of Chinese laborers and sex workers and made exemptions for certain classes such as merchants and diplomats. It also denied all Chinese people the right to become US citizens.

In practice, all Chinese at the border, regardless of their legal status or profession, were treated as suspicious until they could prove they were admissible. Merchants had to show financial records of their businesses. Women had to answer intrusive questions about their sex lives. Family members were separately interrogated about the minutiae of their lives, from the location of the rice bin in the house to the number of steps to the front door. If the stories matched, officers treated the relationship as legitimate; if not, they could be denied entry.

In 1924, Congress passed the Immigration Act, which, among many other things, denied admission to all "aliens ineligible for citizenship." This included foreign-born spouses of Chinese merchants and US citizens. Some women had boarded ships to join their husbands in America before the law was implemented, but when they arrived at Angel Island they found they were not permitted to land. Like the people held at airports this past weekend, these women had followed the rules. Their only crime was their race.

The Chinese Exclusion Act was initially set to expire in ten years. It was renewed for another ten years in 1892, extended without limit in 1902, and finally repealed in 1943, sixty-one years after it passed. If I were born a hundred years ago, I would have been one of the women detained and humiliated at Angel Island, instead of an engaged citizen and participant in America's civic life.

I also knew that my US citizenship is a kind of bulwark. It is not a guarantee of protection—just ask the Chinese American citizens stranded on Angel Island without reentry certificates or the Japanese American citizens interned during World War II. But if I were not a citizen, I would be less invested, more hesitant to speak up about politics.

What is citizenship? It is firstly a legal privilege that we inherit at birth. In most countries, children are automatically given their fathers' citizenship; in most cultures, identity is derived from the father's lineage. Some countries, mostly those in which women have a modicum of equality, also give children their mothers' citizenship. A few countries confer birthright citizenship to children born within their borders to non-citizens. We are citizens of a nation or two by virtue of blood and family, our most primal roots. We define our power and identity by our origins.

To take up citizenship in another country is to *naturalize*: to be made natural, normal. In this framework, to immigrate is to move away from our origins, break with our lineage, and become unnatural and alien, which is aberrant to many who subscribe to the idea of a patrilineal homeland.

For years, my husband pasted images of little green men on the folders in which he kept his immigration paperwork. Even green card holders are not yet normalized: The official term for them is Permanent Resident Alien, each with their own Alien Registration Number. Debates on immigration and citizenship are ultimately debates on race. Who can we consider kin? Who can we make normal?

The Chinese Exclusion Act did not keep out the Chinese. For a fee, Chinese men in America would claim unrelated men in China as their sons. Brokers drew up coaching papers, fictitious family histories that the migrants would memorize on the voyage to America and toss into the sea before entering the San Francisco Bay. If all these claims of family relationships had been true, nine out of ten children of Chinese people in America would have been boys.

But the law was not just about the entry ban. The Chinese Exclusion Act made life difficult for the Chinese, US citizens and non-citizens alike. It legitimized discrimination against them, whether in employment, housing, or the courts.

In 1885, three years after the passage of the exclusion law, white coal miners in Rock Springs, Wyoming rioted and killed at least twenty-eight Chinese residents. A fight broke out between white and Chinese miners over the right to work in a particular room, and a Chinese man was stabbed in the skull. The whites walked off the job, went home for their guns and knives, and marched through the streets to demand that the Chinese leave town. They blocked the bridges to Chinatown, shot at the fleeing Chinese, and when they realized that many Chinese were hiding in their cellars, they burned down their homes. No one was indicted for the murders.

The Rock Springs Massacre was the culmination of a decade of labor unrest and racial hostility in the mines. Ten years before, Union Pacific Coal had brought in Chinese workers to break a strike. But the Chinese Exclusion Act and the demagoguery around it dehumanized the Chinese, creating an atmosphere in which their murder was acceptable. I thought of this following Trump's executive order when a mosque in Texas burned down and a white nationalist shot six people in a Quebec mosque.

Seven years ago, I visited Angel Island for the first time. I rode a ferry across the bay, climbed a steep flight of stairs, and walked along a service road to the immigration station. The sky was clear and I could see for miles around the bay. I remember thinking that unlike those who were held here, I had the freedom to walk where I wished. I also remember thinking that here, the sea is both a border and a vista of possibility. Borders don't always keep people out, but they do keep those of us inside from seeing what is beyond.

Refuge: Rocky Flats, Colorado

I HAVE NOT DECIDED if I want to visit the Rocky Flats Wildlife Refuge northwest of my home in Denver. The site of a plutonium weapons plant that had been shut down because of flagrant safety violations is now a park with ten miles of trails and an elk herd. It was opened to the public in the summer of 2018, after extensive remediation and an ongoing lawsuit to keep it closed. Federal and state environmental officials, ostensibly quoting science, say that the land has been cleaned up and poses no safety risks to visitors. But activists and scientists alike question the methods and reasoning that led to this conclusion. Here I want to ask another question: what does it mean to designate Rocky Flats as a wildlife refuge?

I drove past Rocky Flats for years without realizing it was there. Along Highway 93 between Boulder and Golden, the plains meet the Rocky Mountains. On one side of the road, the orange-red sandstone slabs of the Flatirons stagger toward the sky, flanked by forests of spruce and pine. On the other side of the road is prairie, green in the spring and golden in the summer, rolling toward Denver's skyscrapers in the distance. Farms and open space occupy much of the land; when I lived in Boulder, I often rode my bike to Marshall Mesa—less than ten miles north of Rocky Flats—where I would hop over rocks and cruise on the smooth single track amid a gorgeous tallgrass prairie. I knew that Rocky Flats was in the vicinity. But I did not know exactly where it was until I took a detour onto Highway 128 during an ice storm and saw the Rocky Flats sign.

A little history: Rocky Flats was built in 1951 as a part of the Cold War arms race to produce plutonium triggers for nuclear warheads. Plutonium-239, the isotope most often used in weapons, is highly radio-active and has a half-life of 24,000 years. It is most dangerous when ingested or inhaled. From the beginning, Rocky Flats was rife with safety problems. In 1957 and 1969, plutonium fires broke out in glass boxes and released the toxic chemical into the atmosphere. In the late 1960s and early 1970s, leaks were found in the barrels storing nuclear waste on the site. Nearby rivers and reservoirs tested for elevated levels of tritium, a radioactive isotope of hydrogen that is a byproduct of plutonium fission. As a result of these revelations, Congress authorized the purchase of a buffer zone around the plant.

Beginning in the late 1970s, environmental and peace activists began to stage demonstrations at Rocky Flats. Poet Allen Ginsberg, who taught at the Naropa Institute in Boulder, and his partner Peter Orlovsky were among the thousands of people who, in an attempt to stop trains carrying nuclear waste from leaving the plant, sat on the tracks in protest. Separately, the Department of Justice and the Environmental Protection Agency investigated the facility for violating environmental laws. On June 6, 1989, FBI agents entered Rocky Flats on the pretext of discussing a potential terrorist threat. Instead, they served plant officials with a search warrant.

The FBI uncovered brazen instances of environmental crimes at Rocky Flats, including water and soil contamination. Traces of plutonium were found in, among other places, pipes and air vents, evidence that the carcinogenic compound was not properly handled. In 1992, after a special grand jury investigation, plant operator Rockwell International was fined $18.5 million, which, at that time, was the largest penalty paid for environmental infractions. The raid, compounded by the fall of the Berlin Wall in 1989, led to the closure of the plant. The buildings were dismantled and the waste was shipped to the Nevada Test Site and the Waste Isolation Pilot Plant in New Mexico.

Remediation of the land began in the 1990s as the plant wound down its operations. Officially, the buffer zone is deemed fully cleaned up; in 2007, the EPA took it off its National Priorities List. Some of the contaminated soil and concrete is buried in the Central Operable Unit, the site of the former plant, unlikely to be suitable for human habitation for thousands of years. In 2001, Congress passed the Rocky Flats National Wildlife Refuge Act, which, as the name states, designated the buffer zone as a protected area. For nearly two decades, due to the lack of adequate funding, the US Fish and Wildlife Service closed the refuge to the public. It finally opened last summer. The official website touts the land as a habitat for the threatened Preble's meadow jumping mouse.

Before Rocky Flats reopened as a sanctuary for nature lovers, Denver Public Schools joined six other school districts in the state to ban field trips to the site, citing the health risks to children. Five environmental groups, including the Rocky Mountain Peace and Justice Center, revived a lawsuit to stop the construction of trails at Rocky Flats, claiming that the cleanup efforts have not been sufficient. The lawsuit is pending, but a judge has rejected the request to bar the public from the trails. Carl Spreng, the Rocky Flats program manager at the Colorado Department of Public Health and Environment, dismissed these concerns as "anti-nuclear" "scare tactics." USFWS Ranger Cindy Souders said that the public should have access to this "xeric tallgrass prairie which is one of the most unique ecosystems of this type in North America."

As I wade through these news reports, I realize that I don't have the scientific expertise to assess whether I want to take the risks of walking in Rocky Flats. Indeed, an array of environmental management agencies have declared the site safe for public access, finding, more specifically, that the potential radiation exposure of visiting the refuge does not exceed acceptable levels. Science may be an objective method, but the questions we ask and the interpretations we draw from experiments and laboratory tests can be clouded by blind spots and biases. After all, for decades government scientists denied the connection between radioactive fallout and heightened cancer risk, even in the face of overwhelming anecdotal evidence. It did not occur to them to connect these dots into data; they willfully or negligently refused to consider this question.

And it seems to me that the backlash to the wildlife refuge is driven by this betrayal. Workers and citizens have been repeatedly lied to about the safety of the plant when it was in operation; why should they believe the government this time that the land poses little risk to visitors? In contrast to the half-life of Plutonium-239, nuclear technology has not been around long enough for us to understand its long-term effects on the land if remediation is even possible. For this reason, many environmental justice advocates want Rocky Flats to lay fallow, set apart from further human activity. By opening the land to the public, we are effectively saying that it is now safe, that the environmental damage has been reversed; by keeping it closed, we remind ourselves that the dangers of the plutonium weapons plant cannot be easily erased.

Consider the *Oxford English Dictionary* definition of the word *refuge:* "shelter or protection from danger or trouble." We think of refuge as a place of safety, a retreat from the ills of the world, and *wildlife*, again from the *OED:* "the native flora and fauna of a particular region." The blueprint for Rocky Flats is the Rocky Mountain Arsenal National Wildlife Refuge about twenty miles due east on the other side of Denver, the site of a former chemical weapons plant that is now home to a buffalo herd. Especially in this age of technology, we see wildlife as a primordial life force, an ancient connection to the rhythms of the earth. There may be a Rocky Flats Cold War Museum fifteen miles away in Arvada and interpretive signs along the trails to remember this history, but on some level, in calling Rocky Flats a wildlife refuge, even if technically correct, even if the elk herd continues to thrive, we are minimizing what had happened here.

The Ghosts of Bitter Creek

I AM NOT ONE who sees ghosts, but the first time I drove through Rock Springs, Wyoming, I had a sense that the area was haunted. I was in my early twenties, a few years into my life in Denver and the American West, on the road to the sublime peaks and geysers of the Tetons and Yellowstone. I had figured that Rock Springs was just another forgotten town in the bleak expanse of desert scrub on the way to paradise, and if I did not have to exit Interstate 80 and skirt the town onto Highway 191, I might have sped past it, the hills of sagebrush and broken rock only a blur in my peripheral vision. But I had to slow down onto the exit ramp. I made a quick stop at a gas station. I was not paying attention to my surroundings, thinking instead of the next four or five hours I had on the road. Yet I felt a nebulous presence, a shadow that I could not shake off.

A year after that drive through Wyoming, I visited the detention center at Angel Island for the first time. I walked in the barracks that is now a museum, along the crowded rows of bunk beds stacked three high, looking at the cold waters of the San Francisco Bay where the morning fog was beginning to lift. All around me on the walls were the faded inscriptions of poems some of the Chinese detainees had carved into the wood. I saw that without this history of exclusion and detention, these views would have been exalted for their wild beauty. But here the sea was designed to be a barrier to escape; this sublime landscape also reinforced the brutality of America's immigration policies. I did not know how to go about it yet, but I knew I was going to write about Angel Island and the histories of Chinese immigrants in the American West.

As I delved into the history of Chinese exclusion, I learned about what happened at Rock Springs: on September 2, 1885, white coal miners rioted, killed at least twenty-eight Chinese men, and drove the rest of the Chinese out of town at gunpoint. The strange feeling that I had in Rock Springs came back to me. In traditional Chinese culture, it is believed that if a person is not given the proper burial rites, their spirit would roam the land until they could find their way home. The bodies of most of the men who were murdered in Rock Springs would not have been repatriated, especially if only fragments of their bones were found in the rubble of their dugouts after the mob set Chinatown on fire. Maybe it was their presence that I had felt.

The Rock Springs Massacre was the result of ten years of labor struggles in the Union Pacific coal mines. The company had built the transcontinental railroad through southern Wyoming in part because these basin and rangelands comprised the least difficult area to cross the high peaks of the Rockies, in part because the Pacific Railway Act gave the railroad land grants along the lines it built, and the land around Rock Springs was rich in coal. The railroad transformed this landscape. All the major towns along Interstate 80, Laramie, Rawlins, Rock Springs, Evanston—Cheyenne is an exception—are about a hundred miles apart. All of them began as railroad stops. Rock Springs owes its existence to the railroad, which brought workers to the town and shipped coal away from the mines. The welcome arch downtown still says, "Home of Rock Springs Coal."

In 1874, developer and financier Jay Gould bought a controlling stake in the Union Pacific. The company had been floundering under the massive loans it took out to finance the construction of the transcontinental railroad. Although the Rock Springs mines were the most profitable segment of the company, Gould slashed the miners' wages. The next year, the Union Pacific cut wages again and, adding insult to injury, demanded a 25 percent increase in production to keep up with the winter demand. That November, the miners, most of whom were from Britain or Scandinavia, walked out. When negotiations reached an impasse, the

Union Pacific brought in 150 Chinese workers from California to break the strike. The US Army was called in to protect the Chinese. The company then fired the strikers and rehired white miners on the condition they sign an ironclad that they would not join a union or strike again.

The first Chinese had come to America during the California gold rush. Most of these early immigrants were young men from Canton, and they often left behind wives and children as they ventured abroad to strike it rich. Some of them were sent to Latin America, especially Peru and Cuba, as indentured laborers, worked to death in the mines and on plantations that once tortured African slaves. Some borrowed money to come to the United States, where a portion of their paychecks went to pay off the debt on their Pacific passage. Many of these lucky ones worked on the Central Pacific, the western half of the transcontinental railroad, across the steep grades of the Sierra and the parched flats of the Nevada desert.

These Chinese laborers built the most difficult stretch of the railroad. Not only did they tunnel through the granite of the high Sierra, but they did so during some of the worst winters on record in these mountains, sleeping in snow sheds and risking explosions and avalanches so the railroad would be finished on schedule. The Summit Tunnel alone, located at Donner Pass, took more than a year to build, with many lives lost to falling debris, mistimed nitroglycerin blasts, and rumbles of snowpack unable to hold. The white men in Congress and the railroad barons might have supplied the capital and the political will to sustain the project, but it was the Chinese who broke their bodies to get the job done.

The completion of the transcontinental railroad in 1869 put many workers, white and Chinese alike, out of work. The Panic of 1873 further depressed wages and increased unemployment. That September, Jay Cooke and Company, which had been overleveraged on Northern Pacific Railway bonds, declared bankruptcy and sparked a bank panic so severe that the New York Stock Exchange halted trading for ten days. The Chinese were already seen as alien and unable to assimilate, but during these years of economic privation, the rhetoric against them turned violent. The Chinese took away jobs. They were willing to work for lower wages. They were, as a headline in Denver's *Rocky Mountain News* described in October 1880, a month before a race riot broke out there and one Chinese man was lynched, "The Pest of the Pacific Coast" and "The Heathen Who Have Ruined California."

In addition, Chinese women were seen as threats to the integrity of American families. Most wives stayed in China to take care of the children and in-laws as their husbands worked abroad. But with a large population of lonely men in America, there was a demand for sex workers. Many women were tricked with the promise of a wealthy husband in America, and in some cases, they were outright kidnapped. When they arrived in San Francisco, they were sold to brothels, where they had to work without pay for at least four years to pay back the cost of their voyage. In 1875, in response to a moral outcry, Congress banned the entry of Chinese sex workers. In practice, it meant that wives who wanted to join their men in America had to submit to humiliating interviews with American consular officers about their sex lives, deterring their desire to emigrate. As a result, most Chinese women in America in the late 1800s were indeed in the sex trade, painted both as temptresses who wrecked the innocence of good white boys as well as silenced victims of a terrible racket.

A popular chant in labor rallies, including the one in San Francisco in July 1877 that erupted into a city-wide race riot, was "The Chinese Must Go!"

In 2014, I went to Rock Springs for a few days to research the story of the Chinese Massacre. When I was there, riots broke out in Ferguson, Missouri, after Black teenager Michael Brown Jr. was fatally shot by a white cop. In Wyoming, I spent my days in the archives and museum exhibits, trying to understand that day more than a century ago when people who looked like me were murdered and driven out of town. I walked along Bitter Creek, the alkaline wash that runs through town, flooding in the spring and drying up this late in the summer. I drove to the Reliance Tipple just outside of town, one of the few surviving relics of the old coal days, and looked into its cavernous passageways from behind a fence, trying to parse the rage and sorrow of the men who worked there. I drove to Green River, the next town west whose namesake is the major tributary of the Colorado River, where the rioters who were arrested in the aftermath of the massacre were hauled into the Sweetwater County jail. I drove further west to Evanston, a town near the Utah border with a joss house that is now a museum, where the Chinese who fled into the hills on that cold September night were dropped off by Union Pacific trains sent to their rescue. I took a joyride down to the Flaming Gorge Reservoir, the first of many dams on the Green River, its turquoise waters strangely beautiful amid the red sandstone walls. Back in Rock Springs, I took in tales of the iconic outlaws Butch Cassidy and Calamity Jane, both of whom briefly lived in this town. I grabbed a beer and danced at the Sweetwater Blues n' Brews Festival at Bunning Park. At night, I returned to my motel room and watched the aftermath of a racially motivated slaying unfold on television.

Rock Springs does not try to hide its brutal racial history, but it does not wear it on its sleeve either. The town museum has an exhibit on the Chinese Massacre that tells this story evenhandedly, that of a labor struggle that turned into a deadly riot. All the museum and library staff were more than happy to talk to me about my research, though when I sent inquiries before I came, their responses were often addressed to "Mr. Goh." I am not sure if they simply defaulted to the male pronoun or if they thought, subconsciously or otherwise, that men were more likely to be interested in this story of economic and racial violence. In any case, I was not sure how the locals would regard a Chinese city girl on a mission to write about the skeletons in the town's closet, but even the waitstaff and an old-time trona miner I met at the brewery were eager to tell me about the old Chinatown. But the Miner's Memorial bears no Chinese names.

I also learned that some of the diners right off the interstate serve "American Chinese" cuisine: burgers and chicken fried steak on one side of the menu, chow mein and kung pao chicken on the facing page.

The most prominent story that I found in Rock Springs, as prominence goes in southwestern Wyoming, is that Butch Cassidy once lived here and even did time in the town jail. Cassidy was a bank and train robber and leader of an outlaw gang in the Old West whose exploits are immortalized in Paul Newman and Robert Redford's 1969 film *Butch Cassidy and the Sundance Kid*. It is also rumored that Calamity Jane had a dugout in Rock Springs. She was a hard-drinking, sharpshooting, trousers-wearing frontierswoman who told tales of her exploits in Indian campaigns and dalliances with other outlaws—though not Cassidy—that were as tall as the myths that shrouded her life. Like Cassidy, her story has been recounted in several Hollywood westerns, romanticized and likely fictionalized to fit a role, that of the cowboy—or cowgirl—who lives on the fringe of society and defies social mores in favor of a higher sense of honor.

The cowboy remains a potent icon in American culture and especially in conservative politics. Three of the last four Republican presidents and presidential candidates were framed as tough-going, straight-talking outsiders, even though a cursory look at their backgrounds reveal lives fully embedded in the corridors of power: Donald Trump the anti-establishment billionaire, John McCain the flyboy Maverick, and George W. Bush—well, he literally dressed up as a cowboy, complete with a Texas ranch. (Mitt Romney's suits are too well-cut for him to even try to play cowboy.) The fact that all these men are scions of powerful families matters less to their base than the emotional appeal of their gestures, the ideals of freedom and individualism they sought to embody.

Hollywood situates the cowboy as the origin story of the American West, an emblem of stoic masculinity, of power derived from the ability to control one's emotions and environment. In actuality, the cowboy myth had been formed in reaction to the closing of the frontier. The frontier represented the opportunity to start over again, creating a new self that is free from social impositions, at least for the white men and women who saw themselves as pioneers and settlers. The 1890 Census showed few tracts of unpopulated land left in the West, few places left to serve as an escape valve, which sparked anxieties about what it meant to be American, about the direction the nation was taking. The cowboy held onto this promise of freedom. More than that, he was also a mask for the real forces that shaped the West: the corporations and industrial robber barons, and in particular, the railroads.

Gold might have brought seekers from around the world to the heights of the Sierra and the Rockies, but it was the railroad that made travel across the mountains and deserts much more possible and practicable, connecting the frontier to the power centers of the East. And the railroads were the first modern corporations. The Southern Pacific, successor to the Central Pacific, was known as the Octopus, for its tentacles in many industries, controlling freight rates, commerce, and even settlement patterns. The more I delve into these histories, the more I see that the transcontinental railroad is the real origin story of the American West, its force and ingenuity the ultimate realization of Manifest Destiny. The charismatic and down-home cowboy is a cloak for this ideology of dominance, this white supremacy.

The Chinese were among the first people who were compelled to emigrate at the beginning of the industrial era, leaving impoverished towns and ruined crops to provide backbreaking labor in a foreign land, a prefiguration to today's global displacements. For the most part, they were not slaves, not in North America at least. Instead, they inhabited a liminal space with the illusion of choice, free to accept or break contracts, their lives still constrained by the circumstances of their race and origins. They were the antithesis of the cowboy, stereotyped as meek and subservient, unable to reinvent themselves, a visible representation of the underbelly of industrial capitalism that the nation would rather not acknowledge. Chinese exclusion may have been driven by tribalism and xenophobia, but it was also a backlash to the degradations of a newly mechanized world.

On a return trip to Rock Springs for more research, I visited the Chinese Joss House Museum in Evanston. There I found the story of an independent Chinese woman who moved to the area with the arrival of the railroad. Her real name remains unknown; like most Chinese women in the sex trade, she was simply called China Mary. She helped many of the men who ended up in Evanston with little more than the clothes on their backs after the massacre. She not only survived the Wild West without a madam or man in a time when there were few opportunities for Chinese women, but she also lived to over a hundred years old. I had been trying to create a sex worker character to tell part of the story through the lens of a Chinese woman. It turned out that the particulars I had conjured from my research into Chinese women in the Old West—which tended to focus on San Francisco, where most of them lived—mirrored China Mary's life as if I had been channeling a ghost.

When the COVID-19 pandemic shut everything down and I had to stay at home, I took out the handful of poems I had written over the years and hunkered down to finish the book. As I wrote about the actions and rhetoric that shaped that horrific day in 1885, then-President Donald Trump was openly blaming China for the virus, calling it the "China virus" and "kung-flu." As a result, in this past year and counting of the pandemic, anti-Asian sentiments have resurfaced with a vengeance. Asians have been beaten up on the streets in the United States and around the world, much like in Wyoming in summer 1885, when white miners in Rock Springs saw Colorado miners successfully take on the Union Pacific and blamed the Chinese for their inability to strike, for their impotence.

I remember a week when I was trying to figure out how I wanted to tell China Mary's story in that tense summer of 1885. That week, a young white man opened fire on three Asian spas in Atlanta, killing eight people and wounding one. Six of the victims were Asian women, mostly middle-aged to elderly working-class Koreans with limited English trying to eke out lives on the margins of society. The shooter claimed he was grappling with sex addiction and saw the massage parlors as sources of temptation that he had to eradicate. The Chinese Exclusion Act may have been repealed in 1943, but the forces that shaped that era are still with us. The stereotypes remain the same—Asians are obedient robots and Asian women are submissive sirens—convenient specters to invoke in times of cataclysmic change, in times of anxiety about what the future might hold.

I don't believe in ghosts. But as I worked on these poems, I felt another kind of presence, that of the people who are not represented in the archives. The material I collected includes newspaper clippings, payroll and arrest records, telegrams between the Union Pacific and the Wyoming territorial government, a report on the causes of the massacre commissioned by the Union Pacific, interviews with white miners suspected of being rioters, and a handful of eyewitness accounts. The documents contain evidence, but the deeper story lies in the lives of the people who haunt these official reports, the intimate terrain beneath the facts. And the archives tell this story from a white perspective, slanted toward the interests of the railroad managers and territorial government. It is the story told by those in power to deflect their culpability in this atrocity.

There are no known records left by the Chinese men who worked on the railroads and in the mines of the Old West, be it the builders of the Central Pacific or the miners in Rock Springs—no letters and no journals in China or the United States. The best knowledge we have of the Chinese who lived in Wyoming comes from archaeological digs in the areas around Rock Springs and Evanston, which grants some insight into the material conditions of their lives. Though many of them lived in crowded shacks, especially in the section camps outside of the two larger towns, they also imported luxuries such as dried oysters and abalone into the desert. And in one of my favorite passages from these reports, historian and researcher A. Dudley Gardner writes,

> Remains of alcoholic-beverage bottles manufactured in the United States indicate more than a casual consumption of goods originating in America. The use of alcohol, no matter what the brand or type, may have had less to do with cultural preferences than the desire for a drink or the inability to differentiate between high-quality liquor and bad liquor once a certain level of consumption was reached.

To write about the Rock Springs Chinese Massacre, I needed to figure out the official story first, the version backed by document and evidence, biased as it is. I needed to elucidate the white accounts of the American West. It is the scaffolding I had to build so I could see the gaps in the narrative, the silences of erasure and decay. In conveying the perspectives of white miners and officials, I am not so much capitulating to their point-of-view, but rather I am drawing attention to the beliefs and rhetoric that shape their actions and the forces of history that add up to one of the worst episodes of anti-Chinese violence in the United States. At the same time, I imagined the voices of the people who lived in these gaps. I used what we know about these Chinese migrant workers, together with my knowledge of Chinese culture and beliefs, to fill in the story from their perspectives. This work may be fleshed out from my imagination, but it is also rooted in historical facts.

This is not my story, in the sense that I am not descended from these pioneer Chinese, but I see now that they made it possible for newcomers like me to live in the American West, embrace these wild landscapes, and complicate our understanding of this place I have come to call home. I joke that I should write a story set in Paris instead, but here in the desolate West, I can do my small part to shift the narrative away from individual freedoms and consider this history in a global context of exclusion and domination. As I roam in the archives and sagebrush hills of Wyoming, I see that I am also writing an origin story for the Chinese in America, a story that reexamines our myths of the American West, a story I hope will explode our vision of who belongs in this unruly nation.

Home Lands

WHAT DOES IT MEAN for an immigrant to be at home?

Home, we are taught, is about our origins. It is where we are born and raised. It is a sense of belonging that may be true for many people, but it has also been weaponized against immigrants. For if home is where you were born, then to migrate is to never be at home, to never have stakes— and if you have never set down meaningful roots, then it becomes easy to justify removing you.

"Go home!" we yell at people we think do not belong, who don't look like us, even if this is where they have lived for decades, even if they were born here.

*

Immigration is always about race. You can't tell a person's legal status just by looking at them, but you can tell if they belong to a targeted race. Between 1882 and 1943, when the Chinese Exclusion Act was in place, all Chinese people, including US citizens, had to carry papers to prove that they were legally in the country. Similarly, all Chinese people at the ports of entry had to make sure they had the right documents to land, including affidavits from white associates, even if they were US citizens.

The color of their skin was enough to question the validity of their papers, their claims to America as home.

In 1895, immigration officers at the Port of San Francisco denied reentry to Wong Kim Ark, a man born in the United States to Chinese immigrant parents. Under the Citizenship Clause of the Fourteenth Amendment, by virtue of his birth on US soil, he was automatically conferred birthright citizenship. But under the Chinese Exclusion Act, all Chinese people were considered ineligible for naturalization. The immigration officers argued that Wong, as a child of Chinese immigrants, was a Chinese subject even though he was born in the United States. They held him on steamships off the coast of San Francisco for five months as his lawyers argued his case before the courts. His case eventually reached the US Supreme Court in 1898 as *United States v. Wong Kim Ark*, which ruled in his favor. But his ancestry was enough to question whether he had the right to return to his home.

This ugly primacy of ancestry over citizenship reared its head again in World War II when President Franklin Roosevelt issued an executive order that allowed the military to designate exclusion zones in the name of national security. On paper, the order did not specifically mention Japanese-Americans, but in effect, all people of Japanese descent, including US citizens—who, due to the exclusion laws of the time, were largely US-born children of Japanese immigrants—were subject to forcible removal from their homes and sent to internment camps. The justification to include US citizens was the belief that they would be more loyal to Japan than America, that blood would trump the lived and made existence. In other words, not only can an immigrant never be at home, but neither could their US-born and bred descendants.

*

In 2016, we elected a president who ran on a platform of overt xenophobia. I don't care for the man himself; I care about the brutal consequences that his actions and rhetoric have on people's lives. He did not invent xenophobia, but he tapped into a vein of fear and resentment that is as old as the founding of America and styled himself as its most prominent spokesperson. Back in 2015, he announced his candidacy by portraying immigrants from Mexico as hordes of criminals and rapists and promised that he would build a wall on the southern border.

This border was created by the Treaty of Guadalupe-Hidalgo in 1848, which ended a war that began when white Anglo settlers believed that the seemingly uninhabited lands of the continent were theirs for the taking, including land that belonged to Mexico. As part of the agreement, Mexico ceded large parts of California, Nevada, Arizona, Utah, Colorado, New Mexico, and Texas to the United States. Many Spanish-speaking communities in the borderlands have never crossed the border; the border crossed them. In addition, for a number of Native American peoples such as the Tohono O'odham, the border splits their homelands in two, an artificial boundary imposed on them. For decades after the creation of the border, people moved freely across it, whether for seasonal work, family visits, or a sense of adventure. They continued to do as they had been doing all along; after all, this land is a contiguous mass with peoples, cultures, and social relationships that predated the arrival of the Anglo-Europeans.

In 1965, Congress passed the Immigration and Nationality Act, a package of comprehensive immigration reforms for the time. Between 1924 and 1965, US immigration operated on a system of quotas by national origin; each country was allowed up to 2 percent of its population in the United States as recorded in 1890. This system was deliberately created to favor the white Anglo-Europeans who dominated the United States in the late 1800s and suppress the entry of Italians and Eastern Europeans. (The Immigration Act of 1924 took care of the number of Asians by banning them outright. When the Chinese Exclusion Act was repealed in 1943, the Chinese were allocated a quota of one hundred immigrants per year.) The 1965 bill did not abolish the quota system altogether, but it created a preference system for families of US citizens as well as a work visa program with a path to citizenship for skilled professionals. In particular, it expanded immigration from Asia, especially for the professional class.

Before 1965, there were no numerical limits on immigration from the Western Hemisphere. Much of the migration across the southern border was informal. Many people, mostly men, crossed the border for seasonal work, drawn by the higher pay in the United States, intending to return to their families during the off-season. Crossing the border has never been easy, but the border was more of a formality then. But in a compromise with white supremacist forces who opposed the reforms of the 1965 bill, Congress added numerical restrictions on immigration from the Western Hemisphere for the first time. And the quota they set was too low and did not account for the social and economic relationships that date back decades, if not centuries. Not surprisingly, it did not stop these informal migrations. Instead, it criminalized this once-free movement of people as illegal immigration.

*

Immigration is one of the few criminal offenses, together with felonies such as murder and rape, that does not have a statute of limitations. That is to say, once you cross the border without the proper documents, it does not matter what you do with the rest of your life. You can build a life here: work an honest job, pay Social Security and Medicare taxes, raise a family, and commit no heinous crimes. All that does not matter. The life for which you have worked hard and the people you love, the children who depend on you for food and shelter, do not matter. There are a few ways out—most notably, a child born in the United States can sponsor you the moment they turn twenty-one—but that would still require two decades of hiding in the shadows, and anti-immigration extremists have been arguing that despite *Wong Kim Ark*, the US-born children of undocumented immigrants should not be granted birthright citizenship as their parents' presence in the country is a crime. If you get caught, you can be deported. Reentry will be considered a felony. And you have to wait ten years to apply for any legal status for which you may qualify. This is not your home.

Or say that your parents brought you across the border when you were five, a decision in which you had no say. You go to school here. You make friends here. You may have younger siblings who were born here and thus are US citizens. You may not remember much of the place where you were born. You may not speak the language well. You may not know anyone there, especially if your extended family has also left. What options for work and college do you have when you graduate high school? What dreams are you permitted to have? The Obama-era Deferred Action for Childhood Arrivals program might have given you some reprieve, a work permit and temporary authorization to stay in the United States, but there is no guarantee that the program will be renewed. Already the Trump Administration has tried to rescind it, but for now, the courts have blocked him. There is still no path to citizenship. Your life is dependent on the winds of politics, rather than on your own skill and will. If the winds blow in the wrong direction, you can get sent "back" to a country that you hardly even know. This is not your home.

*

There are two kinds of power: the kind you inherit and the kind you earn. Monarchy is the ultimate inherited power; your position in society is based entirely on the circumstances of your birth, right down to the birth order in your family. And to state the obvious, the white anti-immigrant zealots who call the United States home are descendants of immigrants if you trace their family trees far back enough—like they did for the Chinese during the Chinese exclusion era and for the Japanese during World War II. But by virtue of their cultural and political dominance, they get to call this land home. The rest of us are immigrants.

For the most part, citizenship is an inherited power. Where you were born and to whom you were born determine which nations will automatically grant you citizenship. And as Eduardo Galeano writes, "The powerful who legitimize their privileges by heredity cultivate nostalgia." If your power and privilege are rooted in the idea of an exclusive homeland, you would want to secure the borders of that land. It is your home, after all, a sentimental place where you can feel safe and protected, where you can nurture your children. A person who crosses this border becomes a threat—a threat to your sense of identity and belonging and thus safety.

This is why the portrayal of Mexican immigrants as gangsters and rapists took hold so easily.

This is why pundits on the "family values" right did not flinch when the Trump Administration instituted family separation policies that put children in cages without their parents, sleeping on floors and without blankets, disallowed to have toys, toothpaste, or even hugs from social workers. In fact, some of them argued these parents had relinquished their parental rights when they put their children through the dangers of the border.

When we make immigration difficult, we are telling people that their blood and ancestry are more important than their abilities.

We are telling people that no matter how hard they work, they can never earn the safety and protection of home.

Fire Season

August 9, 2020

On the road from Steamboat Springs back to Denver, my husband and I decide to avoid the traffic on Interstate 70 and take a joyride across North Park, a remote mountain basin in northern Colorado, and down Poudre Canyon to Fort Collins before heading south to Denver. That weekend, it is unusually hot, even in the mountains. In Steamboat Springs, famed for the plentiful snow that attracts skiers in the winter, the Yampa River has slowed to a trickle, closed to paddlers.

Locals say that it rarely gets this warm in town.

As I drive up Cameron Pass toward the Continental Divide, between the Medicine Bow and Never Summer Mountains, I remember my first winter camping trip here more than a decade ago, playing in the snow and cooking chicken curry in a yurt. For the heck of it, some of us built a snow cave and slept in it for a night. This time around, despite the name of the mountain range, there is hardly any snow on the peaks.

Down the canyon, the Poudre River is no higher than the Yampa. Usually, there are buses full of tourists going whitewater rafting, but the water is so low, perhaps ankle-deep, that it would be difficult for boats to navigate the rocky bed. There are only two or three rafts on the water.

We see the unmistakable burn from the High Park Fire in 2012. Stands of charred trees along both sides of the canyon. Saplings are beginning to grow again, the promise of new life, of renewal. I remember where I was the day that fire started: I was hiking to Chasm Lake, an alpine lake at the base of Longs Peak, the highest point in Colorado. On the way back, we saw massive plumes of smoke and quipped about a nuclear detonation. It took nearly a month to contain that fire. I remember there was a day when the winds were so extreme that the fire jumped the canyon.

August 13, 2020

A fire starts near Cameron Pass.

The Cameron Peak Fire is overshadowed by two larger fires in western Colorado. The Pine Gulch Fire near Grand Junction started on July 31 and will quickly become the largest fire in the state's history, a record that it will hold for seven weeks. The Grizzly Creek Fire in Glenwood Canyon started on August 10 and has closed Interstate 70. The highway will not reopen until August 24.

The Pine Gulch Fire, I see when I look it up on a map, is near Douglas Pass, where a fossil hunt turned into a kitten rescue two years ago. The desert between the mountains and valley will protect the farm in Loma where a friend and I saw a Free Kittens sign and picked up three adorable torbie kittens. We called them the Sand Kittens, for their resemblance to the wild desert cats, and I adopted one of them.

August 14, 2020

The Williams Fork Fire starts in Grand County, near the ski town of Winter Park, about two hours west of Denver.

August 16, 2020

With four wildfires burning in the state, I suppose that it may not have been the best day to hike in Rocky Mountain National Park. But the sky is clear this morning, the winds calm, and a friend and I decide to proceed with our plans to hike the western half of the Ute Trail. Most of this trail is exposed, high in the alpine tundra with views for miles around, and dips into the trees for a bit before it reaches the road again.

At the Alpine Visitor Center, we can see the smoke from the Cameron Peak Fire, which is about twenty miles away.

It turns out that we are right under the flight path for the firefighting aircraft, and we watch air tankers and reconnaissance planes swoop low, barely clearing the peaks. I joke that our pictures can be captioned "Alpine Tundra with Firefighting Airshow."

In the afternoon, the winds switch direction, and we walk back to the car in thick smoke. I take a picture of a marmot that I call "Marmot with Wildfire Smoke." We thought to linger in the park and climb some of the overlooks along the road, but when we get back to the visitor center, we find that the rangers have closed it early because of the poor visibility and air quality.

*

For me, August 16 was the turning point of a summer that began in lockdown because of the COVID-19 pandemic. I am one of the lucky ones: I still had a job that I could do from home. And I don't have children and the attendant upheaval in school or daycare schedules. Lockdown, then, was more of an existential conundrum than a mortal threat. Even for an introvert, staying at home all day started to get old quickly.

At one point, I joked we were all becoming cats, looking out of our windows at the dangerous but alluring world, dreaming that we were roaming out there.

It is one thing to be in the thick of a disaster. It is another to be within its sphere but not quite affected or to be affected in ways that are more of an inconvenience than a grave risk to life. I knew COVID-19 to be a real threat. I watched the news about the rising caseloads and the callous cruelty and mismanagement of the federal response. But I was not on the frontlines. I was not a healthcare or grocery store worker. I could avoid putting myself in the path of risk. The pandemic affects us all, but it affects some people much more than others, and I am one of the privileged ones who get to watch it unfold from the comfort of my home.

From the beginning, I mitigated the cabin fever by taking solo walks outside my home, heading to the neighborhood parks after work, and exploring the nearby open spaces on the weekends. I saw the foothills bloom in the spring and fade into gold in the summer. After the close-in work of looking at a screen all day, gazing at a distance, whether from the mountains to the plains or simply across the street, is a relief. But at the beginning of fire season, as temperatures climbed, humidity fell, and smoke filled the air, I could not go outside either.

I live in an urban part of Denver, which means that a wildfire would have to ravage at least half the city before it gets to me. When I lived in Boulder, I was closer to the mountains, but even in the worst fires in the wildlands around town, I never had to prepare to evacuate. In other words, like the COVID-19 pandemic, I was within range but not in the thick of the fires. I watched them unfold in the news and in the sky, my routines changed again to reduce my smoke inhalation, but for the most part, my worry was more about the state of the world than losing everything.

*

Breathe in. Breathe out.

Breathing is a fundamental mechanism of life. We breathe in to take in the oxygen we need to keep our bodies functioning. We breathe out to release the carbon dioxide that is the byproduct of the cellular processes that keep us alive. If we are deprived of oxygen, we begin to asphyxiate. Brain damage and even death can occur within five minutes.

COVID-19 made breathing suspect.

Early on, it was evident that SARS-CoV-2, as the novel coronavirus came to be called, affects the respiratory system. We now know that the virus also affects the vascular system, but in the first few months of the pandemic, it was entirely thought of as a respiratory virus. Given that it was new, we did not know much about it, including how it is transmitted. Initially, scientists thought it spread through the touching of contaminated objects and advised the public to wash hands and disinfect surfaces. It became clear, though, that the virus can survive at least a couple of hours in the air, in the aerosols and droplets that we produce when we cough, sneeze, speak, or simply breathe.

An infected person breathes out virus.

If we are in their vicinity, we are likely to breathe in virus.

To make things worse, it also became clear that a significant number of infected people are asymptomatic; that is, they do not appear to be sick even when they are infectious. That is to say, in the absence of regular population-wide testing, it is near impossible to be certain that any given one of us is not infected and unwittingly spreading the virus.

Suddenly, we could not take the atmosphere in which we live for granted. Every breath we take feels like a game of roulette.

*

Wildfire smoke makes it difficult to breathe. I don't have respiratory issues, but the acrid smell of smoke makes me lethargic. Some days, when the winds blow the smoke toward Denver, it smells as if the wildfire is right outside my door instead of a hundred miles away. Some days, it rains ash in my yard.

*

On Memorial Day, George Floyd died when a white Minneapolis police officer knelt on his neck for almost nine minutes. Floyd had been arrested for allegedly passing a counterfeit twenty dollar bill. Between the inequalities exacerbated by the pandemic, four years of the Trump Administration and its overt racism, and decades of neoliberal policies that have eviscerated the working class, Floyd's death catalyzed reservoirs of rage into a conflagration.

Street protests erupted across the country. During a time when we were told not to gather in large groups—or any kind of groups—to slow the spread of the coronavirus, people took to the streets to vent at injustice. Many of the Black Lives Matter protestors, in accordance with public health guidelines, wore masks. At the same time, violent groups on the far left and right took advantage of the apparent chaos to burn things down. Cities, including Denver, imposed curfews.

If you look at the pictures without context, it is easy to believe that the country is on fire.

Actually, the country is on fire but not in the ways the news media portrayed it.

This time around, something felt different. Floyd was an individual, but in his death, he also represented the increasingly unbearable cracks in

American society. Even corporations, not exactly beacons of moral progress, felt compelled to take a stand with Black Lives Matter. It does not mean much without actions behind the words, but it indicates a change in the tenor of the conversation. It became impolitic to ignore America's history of devaluing Black lives.

We are not there yet, but social progress is made when previously held prejudices become no longer tenable.

*

Fueled by record-breaking heat and dry winds, the Cameron Peak Fire explodes over Labor Day weekend, going from 24,000 acres on Saturday morning to 102,000 acres by the end of Monday. It turns the sky orange in northern Colorado. A massive snowstorm is forecast for the day after Labor Day, which means that CBS Denver's weather report has FIRE, FREEZE, and SNOW all on the same map of the state, as if hell is going to freeze over. Or that the apocalypse is here.

The storm dumps about fourteen inches of snow on the fire, tamping it down for a few days before dry and windy conditions return again.

The West is on fire. I have lost track of the details of all the blazes in California and Oregon. The day after the snowstorm hit Colorado, the smoke over San Francisco nearly blots out the sun. A friend who lives in East Bay writes to say that lightning lit a brush fire less than a mile from where he lives, in a park where he has taken refuge for exercise in the pandemic, a fire too small to even make the news. This is the fourth straight devastating season in California. In Oregon, fires break out even in the Portland metropolitan area, destroying neighborhoods and causing hundreds of thousands of people to evacuate—and during a pandemic at that.

*

Breathe in. Breathe out.

In 2014, Eric Garner was killed when a Staten Island police officer put him in a chokehold for the alleged sale of untaxed cigarettes. Before he died, he yelled eleven times, "I can't breathe!"

"I can't breathe!" became the rallying cry of the Black Lives Matter movement.

George Floyd also died when he could no longer breathe.

*

At the beginning of the COVID-19 pandemic, the World Health Organization (WHO) and Centers for Disease Control and Prevention (CDC) issued conflicting advice about the efficacy of wearing masks. In part because they worried about a shortage of medical-grade masks for health professionals, a problem exacerbated by breakdowns in the supply chains due to the pandemic, they were initially reluctant to recommend mask-wearing for the general public. But as it became evident that the coronavirus could be spread by droplets and is possibly airborne, the advice became unequivocal: wear a mask.

In many Asian countries, where people commute on overcrowded subways to cramped offices on a regular basis, it is part of the culture to wear a mask when one is ill. Many people also wear masks during the cold and flu season to protect themselves from getting sick. These countries also dealt with the SARS-CoV-1 pandemic in 2003, caused by another coronavirus that is more lethal but somewhat less transmissible than the current one. Given these factors, many people in Asia started wearing masks early on. The idea is simple: a mask is a barrier between your respiratory apparatus and the world.

In some ways, the WHO and CDC bungled their messaging. At first, they said that masks do not protect the general public from the virus. Then they said that non-medical grade masks, which do not filter out particles as small as the virus, are ineffective. By the time they got around to saying that the public should wear cloth masks on top of social distancing, the seeds of doubt and suspicion had already been planted. It did not help that President Trump, who sought to downplay the severity of the pandemic, fanned this distrust by refusing to wear masks, telling his supporters that it is a threat to freedom.

What makes this coronavirus particularly insidious is that it can spread from people who do not know that they are sick, whether they are asymptomatic or have yet to develop symptoms. That is to say, each of us is potentially a vector of harm without knowing it. We can spread the virus by simply breathing and existing in front of other people. The science is clear, but the psychology can be difficult to swallow. Enough people are categorically unable to acknowledge this harm that they can inflict on others, fueling the pandemic.

*

Like COVID-19 and wildfire season, I am not directly affected by police brutality either. As an immigrant woman of color, I might seem like a prime target for the worst excesses of racism, but I also have the financial privilege to mitigate a lot of it. And for better or for worse, Asians, especially those of us in the professional class, are seen as model minorities. I have no illusions about my safety in an all-out race war, but let's put it this way:

If I had children, I would not need to teach them how to avoid drawing the attention of cops or explain to them at a too-young age why a boy who looked like them was killed for playing with a replica toy gun in a park.

If I called the cops on Black or brown people, they would defend me against them.

*

October in Colorado is usually a time for us to hunker down with apple cider or whiskey, watching snow blanket the peaks and dreaming of ski season. This year, it is unseasonably warm. We received no precipitation, whether rain or snow, after the Labor Day snowstorm. All of the state is in the worst drought since 2013.

October 13–14, 2020

The Cameron Peak Fire explodes again. It grows by more than 30,000 acres overnight to about 164,000 acres, surpassing the record the Pine Gulch Fire set seven weeks ago. Most of this growth is on the southeastern flank, racing toward the Big Thompson Canyon and the city of Loveland. A friend who adopted a Sand Kitten evacuates her ranch with two dogs, two cats, and many horses. I cannot help with the horses or dogs, but I offer that if it comes down to it, I can take in the cats so that she would not have to worry about them. It does not come to that, thankfully.

In pictures, the town of Estes Park, the eastern gateway to Rocky Mountain National Park and perhaps best known as the setting for Stephen King's horror novel *The Shining,* looks like it is ringed by orange hills of fire.

From my office in downtown Denver, I watch the smoke come over the mountains and dissipate into the sky. Sunset casts a light pink hue on the plumes.

October 14, 2020

The East Troublesome Fire starts outside of the town of Grand Lake, the western gateway to Rocky Mountain National Park. It barely makes the news.

October 17, 2020

The Calwood Fire breaks out in the foothills above Boulder, causing the town of Jamestown to evacuate. This is not the town's first brush with disaster. In 2013, a thousand-year flood destroyed the road out of Jamestown and residents had to be airlifted to Boulder. Many of the roads north of Boulder are now closed for evacuation. A massive plume of smoke arches from the mountains to the plains, darkening half the sky, now an exhausting sight.

At least it did not create its own thunderstorms, as the Pine Gulch Fire did in the summer.

October 18, 2020

The Lefthand Canyon Fire breaks out in the foothills above Boulder, not far from the Calwood Fire. I cannot keep track of it all.

October 21, 2020

The East Troublesome Fire explodes under high winds to more than 100,000 acres overnight, 6,000 acres an hour. Grand Lake evacuates with little notice in the middle of the night. A couple in their eighties decides to stay to defend their home. They make a last phone call to their children as the flames close in on them; their bodies are found a few days later. A convoy of election officials, escorted by the sheriff's department, drive into town to rescue the ballot box.

October 22, 2020

The East Troublesome Fire races into the west side of Rocky Mountain National Park and spots the Continental Divide. The fire is so ferocious that it jumps across the crest of the Rockies, a land of tundra and scree. It is now less than ten miles from the Cameron Peak Fire and firefighters are worried that the two fires may merge into one gigantic conflagration.

This fire is now the second largest in state history.

With the Thompson Zone of the East Troublesome Fire burning to its west and the Cameron Peak Fire to its north and east, the town of Estes Park is under mandatory evacuation.

Rocky Mountain National Park is closed to visitors.

A massive snowstorm is in the forecast for October 25, but firefighters still have to contend with two more days of low humidity and high winds.

*

Fire is endemic to the forests of the American West. Small fires every fifteen or twenty years clear out the undergrowth and help maintain the ecosystem. When the Anglo-Europeans settled—or conquered—the West, they saw in the land both natural resources to be exploited and virgin wilderness to be preserved. Landscapes such as Yellowstone and Yosemite appealed to Romantic ideas of the sublime and had to be protected from the incursions of industry.

Until recently, we did not understand the role of fires in these forests and sought to suppress them. After all, we saw these forests as untouched and wanted to freeze them in an Edenic state. Fire, in this worldview, is a threat to paradise. For nearly a hundred years, the US Forest Service had a policy in which all fires had to be put out by the morning after they were spotted. Without regular fires, the forests became overgrown. Dead leaves and branches accumulated and became fuel loads, ready to burn.

With the hotter and drier conditions wrought by climate change, these forests are burning out of control.

And much of the forests that the East Troublesome Fire ravaged are pine beetle kill. Like fire, the mountain pine beetle is part of the forest ecosystem. It lays its eggs under the bark and secretes a blue stain fungus that blocks the flow of nutrients in the tree. In this way, it helps to kill off weakened trees and allow the forest to renew itself. Usually, the deep cold of winter halts their reproduction, but with warmer summers and milder winters, the beetles are proliferating and attacking otherwise healthy trees. These dead trees provide more fuel for fires.

*

This season's fires, both literal and metaphorical, stem from our inability to see ourselves as conduits of harm, even if inadvertent.

How do we recognize the invisible harm that we cause others?

*

Breathe in. Breathe out.

The fires came within a mile of Estes Park before a storm dropped more than a foot of snow in the area. The snow did not extinguish the fires, but it tamped them down enough that firefighters could get them under control. As I write in the middle of November, the Cameron Peak Fire is 92 percent contained and the East Troublesome Fire is at 37 percent. The two fires did not merge. We know that Rocky Mountain National Park is damaged, but not to what extent.

The air has cleared up and we are no longer choking on smoke.

The anxiety of this summer was also heightened by the presidential election, and in some ways, we were holding our breath as Donald Trump openly advocated for white supremacy, denied climate change, and bungled the coronavirus response, among too many other things to list. Above all, he and his supporters have a pathological refusal to recognize or acknowledge the harm they cause others. He has been voted out of office, but the fires he fanned still remain, the embers still smoldering, ready to ignite again if the conditions are right.

Already the COVID-19 infection rates have spiked to levels higher than the beginning of the pandemic. The daily number of new cases has reached 100,000, and it is still climbing. It is not yet time to relax. It is going to be a long and terrible winter.

V

Off the Page

The Stories that Bind Us

"WE'D RATHER HAVE SATISFACTION and the maximum titillation than real information," writes Poe Ballantine, "and so history isn't a cold sequential list of facts, it's a prize anthology of the best fiction." I think of Joan Didion's famous adage, "We tell ourselves stories in order to live." Stories shape our worlds. They are, for better or for worse, compasses by which we navigate our lives. Each time we tell a story, we are creating maps of our values and beliefs. We may reinforce what is false and sentimental, or we may tell truths that make us uncomfortable.

We tell stories all the time, even those of us who are not writers. We edit our memories to conform to our beliefs, to try and forget that which is agonizing, to enlarge our moments of great joy or despair. In our stories we tell ourselves who we are and who we can be; in listening to another's story we reach outside the chatter in our heads and inhabit their worlds. We empathize. Isn't love, then, the making of another person's story a part of our own? Similarly, to question another's truth is to question their identity. To erase their stories is an act of cruelty.

To be published is to be in a position of authority. We can influence public opinion. It is a form of power, even though many of us writers often feel—at least I do—that I am only typing before a disembodied screen, my shoulders increasingly knotted, the world drifting by outside my window. And with power comes responsibility. What do we choose to remember and what do we choose to forget? Are we telling a story to satisfy our most craven beliefs or are we trying to unearth a buried truth? Are we reinforcing our prejudices or are we opening our hearts?

True crime meets memoir in Ballantine's *Love and Terror on the Howling Plains of Nowhere*. Steven Haataja, a new math professor at Chadron State College, disappears one winter night and is found three months later, burned and bound to a tree. Like many in his field, he was more comfortable with the abstractions of algebra than with social interactions, though he was not without friends. Between the incompetence of the local police and perceived stereotypes about math recluses, the case remains unsolved and the townspeople speculate, among other things, that Haataja killed himself or was murdered by a disgruntled student, a secret lover, or for being a closet homosexual.

At the time of Haataja's disappearance, Ballantine is in a creative rut. The first time he came to Chadron, a town of 5,000 on the high Plains of northwestern Nebraska, he had dropped out of school and fled a failed romance. The West, he writes, is "the direction of escape after disaster, the direction of decline and the setting sun."

Ballantine had eschewed a conventional life for literature but had nothing to show for it. Mired in feelings of failure, he intended to kill himself. In Chadron, however, as he worked a string of menial jobs, he picked himself up. Years later, when he returned from Mexico with his wife-to-be Cristina, he decided to settle in Chadron for its safety and affordability.

In Mexico, Cristina was a dentist. In America, she works as a maid and janitor. Dependent on her husband to navigate her new country, she fears the loss of her identity, which manifests as fights over petty matters. Ballantine tries but cannot entirely understand, and their arguments escalate. Their child Tom, unexpected but much welcomed, holds the marriage together. At school, he is marked for autism. He cannot relate to the other children, though he is good with adults. He has an exceptional memory, an insatiable curiosity, and often drifts into his own world. Ballantine vows to make the relationship work for Tom's sake.

Cristina had imagined America as a land of unprecedented wealth and sees Ballantine's devotion to literature, with its long hours and abysmal pay, as futile. A private person, she is also uncomfortable with his ethos of self-revelation. A contract with a major publishing house fizzled when he could not get along with the editor and he vows not to work for them again. As he settles down in Chadron, he begins to sell his work to independent presses. (He is best known for his personal essays in *The Sun Magazine*.) Perhaps this is also a great advertorial for the dedication of small press editors: Rhonda, his editor, and her fiancé Kevin fly from Portland, Oregon to Chadron to help him brainstorm ideas for his fifth book.

Rhonda throws up ideas that range from an autism cookbook and a graphic novel about the townspeople to the police beat from the local newspaper, but none appeals to Ballantine. The day she is about to leave, Haataja fails to turn up for class and is reported missing. The police show up at Haataja's house and find everything in order except for his bike. It is below zero that night. Through the grapevine, Ballantine learns that Haataja had bought a bag of charcoal and a bottle of schnapps the night he vanished, both of which were found next to his body. He had also asked for advice on the next semester's textbooks and wanted to know the schedule of the local choir he's a part of: signs, in Ballantine's view, that he was not preparing to just walk away.

Ballantine delves into the mystery, one part out of curiosity, one part afraid there may be a murderer on the loose in his community, one part knowing he has book material on his hands. He sees that he has a "true crime" book in the making, a genre that he is uneasy with, for it is often "an exploitation of another's misery, a callous milking of human misfortune, a picnic round a corpse with plastic forks and all the photographs, the bloody mattress and the poor mangled hookers, and the lonely killer with the funny eye, and as long as it's happening to someone else and there aren't too many psychological 'explanations,' I suppose it's great sport."

As he writes this story, Ballantine knows that he is wandering into murky ethical territory.

And he has his detractors. Haataja's sisters, as he writes in the book, refuse to talk to him, believing him a charlatan who is exploiting their brother's death for profit. A few months before publication, they express these sentiments again on the publisher's website. Some of the townspeople enjoy the book, but in a town where people leave not only their cars unlocked but also the keys in the ignition, Ballantine now has to lock his doors. Loren Zimmerman, a criminal justice professor at Chadron State who tried to seduce Ballantine's wife, has threatened a libel suit for Ballantine's negative portrayal of him, as did the town barber for Ballantine's detail that he has nude magazines in his shop.

In the book, Ballantine quotes Didion, "Writers are always selling somebody out."

For most of us writers, the idea that we profit monetarily from our literary work is often laughable at best, but writers, no matter how underpaid or abject, have the power of the pen. Our version of the story enters the public imagination, gets written into the records of culture. The people in our stories often do not have the platform to make a rebuttal or render their perspective. At the same time, it is difficult to avoid writing about others. Our lives are intertwined with those around us, and to tell our stories, it is often necessary to bring in theirs.

The question is then about fairness. Are we telling others' stories to aggrandize ourselves, or are we coming from a place of love and empathy?

Ballantine tries to understand where each person is coming from, whether his wife with whom he had a language barrier, Haataja's history of depression and suicide, or the old crocodile Zimmerman. He gives space to the variations and versions that compete with his point of view. He expresses doubt instead of certainty. He refrains from sensationalism. He exposes the dysfunctions of the town, but he turns the harshest light on his own flaws and failures. And in weaving Haataja's life and death into the stories of his marriage, his son, and the townspeople, he looks deeply into the ties that bind us and the ways they can be broken.

The Subjective Passions

A DECADE AGO, when I first came to America, I flew from Michigan to Honolulu to meet my family. My grandmother, my mother's mother, came along. We stayed with her brother Allen, who has lived on the island since 1971. One day, he brought us to visit my great-grandmother.

I heard about her when I was growing up. Her meals were legendary. Lunches spilled into dinners. Like most family stories, it is often difficult to separate myth from fact, memory from conjecture, but I seem to have heard this story: the family gathered around the television, a scene in which Hong Kong actor Chow Yun Fat lies naked in a bathtub with the lead actress, and my great-grandmother ranting about a decline in the younger generation's morals. The screenwriting credits brought up Uncle Kenneth, her second son.

When I finally met her, she was ninety-seven, wheelchair-bound, in the late stages of dementia, and living in a nursing home. She recognized only Uncle Allen and the nurse who attended to her. As my grandmother, her eldest child, held her hand, she kept calling out the name of her second child, Grace, who had passed away a decade before. My great-grandmother died a few months after that visit. Somewhere in an album is a photograph of four generations of women in my family in the same frame.

Five years later, I received a letter from Aunt Helen, my grandmother's youngest sister in Atlanta. She had just visited my family in Singapore and when my mother said I was in Denver, she asked for my address. The envelope contained a note, a gift of $200, and some photographs from their visit. I wrote her back and visited her when I was in Atlanta, and we still keep up the occasional correspondence and exchange holiday gifts.

My grandmother cared for my siblings and me when my mother was at work, but what I know of her past largely comes from my mother, who knows only as much as my grandmother has been willing to divulge. She grew up in Gulangyu Island, off the Xiamen coast in southern China. Her mother had been sold to a wealthy family at thirteen or fourteen as a future bride for their son. Her parents fought often and would pit their children against one another. After World War II, her father left them for a mistress in Taiwan.

When the Communists came in 1949, the family fled the island. My grandmother and Aunt Grace, the two eldest children at twenty and seventeen, had left for Singapore to find work the year before. Aunt Helen and Uncle Allen, at fifteen and twelve, had seen the writing on the wall and left in the spring to join their father in Taiwan. That fall, my great-grandmother, her mother-in-law, and the two youngest boys took the last boat out of Gulangyu as the Communist army fired on them.

Their father rented a home in Taipei for his wife, mother, and four youngest children, though he did not live with them again. In the 1970s and 80s, the siblings, married and with their own families, moved to the United States on separate occasions. Uncle Kenneth eventually returned to East Asia, where he made his name as a filmmaker and screenwriter.

A few months after I heard from Aunt Helen, I received an email with the subject "Your Aunt in Denver." Aunt Deborah, Aunt Grace's eldest, is the same age as my mother, and as she put it, they grew up not more than five houses apart from each other. As adults, my mother went to London for graduate school and Aunt Deborah to Honolulu for work, and because of the distance, they lost touch. Aunt Deborah asked if we could meet for dim sum.

She described her "motley crew" as "a balding white guy, a lanky Eurasian boy, and a Chinese woman who looks like your grandmother."

The descriptions were not necessary; when she walked into the crowded restaurant, she picked me out immediately. I cannot say what it was, but I recognized her as family too. Over that lunch, she said that she had moved to Honolulu at the same time as Aunt Helen. She was single; Aunt Helen's husband and sons stayed in Taiwan until she could sponsor their visas. They lived next to each other as they settled into a new country.

Each time I try to write about this legacy, I come up against what I do not know. I am beginning to see that there are things I would never know, but these gaps, for better or for worse, are a part of who I am.

*

Before I began Veronica Gonzalez Peña's novel *The Sad Passions,* I had just finished Junot Díaz's *The Brief Wondrous Life of Oscar Wao,* half of it on a return flight from New York and at the insistent recommendation of a friend who happened to be in the city at the same time. The eponymous character in Díaz's novel is an overweight, awkward nerd, socially outcast and unlucky in love. He immerses himself in science fiction and aspires to be the next Tolkien, but ultimately, he is looking for intimacy and connection to disastrous ends.

In the story, Díaz uses multiple narrators, but it is predominantly told from the perspective of Yunior, Oscar's college friend and sometime lover of his sister Lola. Yunior is Nick Carraway to Oscar's Jay Gatsby. He is close enough to observe the family dynamics and play a part in them, but he is still able to maintain some distance. Years after the final tragedy, he tries to reconstruct his friend's life.

Yunior traces Oscar's story back to the Dominican Republic and the brutality of the Trujillo regime. He admits that he is an unreliable narrator, prone to exaggerations and fiction, but as he digs into this history, he finds gaps that only his imagination can fill. Oscar's grandfather is arrested purportedly for speaking ill of the dictator, which brings on a curse in the subsequent generations. His wife and daughters meet with untimely deaths; only the youngest, Belicia, survives, taken in by a family who mistreats her. As a young woman, she is kidnapped and nearly beaten to death for an affair; after she recuperates, she begins a new life in New Jersey.

In trying to put these pieces together, Yunior finds that he often has to conjecture each person's interiority. In the copious footnotes, Díaz gives, among other things, the context of the Trujillo era, but he is not out to teach or correct history. *Oscar Wao* is a family saga in which history looms large in the private and intimate self, and I came away thinking about how legacies are manifested in the present.

*

"I was born the year Julia was given away," *The Sad Passions* begins. "And though nobody knew it at the time, I was there when it happened; because, as I figure it, our mother, Claudia, was three months pregnant with me when the severance occurred." In this haunting novel, four sisters, Rocio, Julia, Marta, and Sandra, grow up in the shadows of their mother's madness. At sixteen, Claudia elopes with her lover Miguel and wanders in the United States. Miguel cannot settle down; in the lonely nights, Claudia begins to have manic episodes. He puts her through electroshock treatment when she is pregnant with their first child and then abandons her with her mother in Mexico City.

Gonzalez Peña tells the story in interlocking chapters of first-person monologues from each of the four sisters, Claudia herself, and Claudia's sister Sofia. They tell the story in retrospect, circling the same episodes from different perspectives, drawing out their own interiority. In her lucid moments, Claudia can be nurturing toward her daughters. But Rocio, the eldest, often has to make simple soups out of scraps to feed her sisters and herself when Claudia cannot take care of them. And when Claudia inexplicably gives Julia away when the girl is six, the sisters live with the fear that they too could disappear, literally and figuratively.

To tell your truth is to fight your erasure. In giving voice to each of the women, Gonzalez Peña foregrounds their subjectivity. In this environment, love is precarious, identities unstable, and reality slippery; the women each have a stake in telling their versions of the story. All of them struggle with defining a self. Rocio finds refuge in boys and marries young; Julia tries to please and turns to art; Marta rebels and tries to run away, without avail; Sandra, the voice that opens the book, sees herself as Julia's double, without an identity of her own. Gonzalez Peña gives us these competing accounts without judgment and demands that we ask, are they equally valid?

And there is nothing objective about the experience of madness. The line between mania and lucidity is often thin, and, as Sylvia Plath showed in *The Bell Jar*, a psychotic episode can seem rational to its sufferer. Notably, Gonzalez Peña does not attempt to diagnose or categorize Claudia's illness. Instead, she gives us the corporeal experience of living with and around it. Diagnosis is a form of labeling, and to label someone as mad is to take away their voice and their credibility. In resisting this move, in giving Claudia her say, no matter how unreliable, Gonzalez Peña gives her back her agency.

*

In the final chapter, Julia, living alone on Long Island with her dog, surrounded by the detritus of a failed relationship with a famous artist who denigrated her efforts to make art, turns to the photography of Francesca Woodman. In the late 1970s and 80s, Woodman made staged photographs of women's bodies, often her own, some of which Gonzalez Peña reproduces in the text. Of the image on the cover, a woman gripping onto a doorframe as if hanging, she writes, "Will that woman in the doorway be discovered as a hanging, or is she divine, an exhausted spirit, perhaps, only momentarily pausing mid-flight?"

Woodman's work reminds me of the photography of Cindy Sherman and Ana Mendieta, women artists whose self-portraits reclaim the agency of the female body. In *Untitled Film Stills,* Sherman dressed up as characters in movie stills, playing on clichés of femininity. In *Siluetas,* Mendieta created silhouettes of her body in nature and made photographs of these performances. As both photographer and subject, these women shape the representation of their bodies and identities, in contrast to the patriarchal model of a male artist and female model. That is to say, these women take control of the gaze and insist on their subjectivity.

I read *The Sad Passions* on my commute, as I do most of my reading nowadays, and each time I reached my destination, I wanted to stay with the spell Gonzalez Peña cast, these labyrinths of apparitions and absences, these gaps my imagination wanted to fill. The girls in Woodman's photographs embody this spirit, hovering on the verge of disappearance, their bodies anonymous and interchangeable. In these photographs, Julia sees the scars she left on her sisters when she was gone, "that in-between place where you are just a ghost mark, so terrified of finally actually disappearing that somehow you don't allow yourself to ever be fully there at all."

The night I finished the book, I realized I had been holding my breath. I wrote down my first impressions between leaving the office and a midnight airport run, and in the following week, I threw myself back into my own projects, making notes in the interstices of the day and writing furiously at night. In part I had inspiration, but looking back now, I also see that I was vulnerable, scattered, and unable to be fully present. Only when I delved into my work, which deals with America's history of migration and exclusion, could I focus and find a ground beneath my feet.

"The play we see permeating Woodman's work," Julia says, "is a necessary in-between place, the unclaimed transitional space, from which we can actively create our own lives." These gaps are the spaces in which art inhabits, and to contend with our legacies, we have to write into this subjectivity, terrifying as it may be.

Lost and Found:
On Kate Zambreno's *Heroines*

I HAVE BEEN TRYING to write about Kate Zambreno's *Heroines* for months, but each time I find what I have to say inadequate. The book is about many things: the shadow histories of the modernist "mad wives" such as Vivien(ne) Eliot and Zelda Fitzgerald, a memoir of Zambreno's struggles as a trailing spouse and beginning writer, a subjective mode of criticism, a reconsideration of the canon, and a battle cry for women to write our true experiences. As a historian, critic, and woman who writes outside of institutional structures, I could ramble on these subjects.

The title of my first draft: *A Work of Her Own*. Reacting to the way women like Vivien(ne) and Zelda were not allowed to work, whether for pay or on their art. I have a job and carve out time to write, which comes from years of compromise and discipline, and yet I often feel that my independence is provisional, that my voice may one day be taken from me.

My second working title: *Her Story*. Excavating the ways women's voices are devalued and dismissed. Even though I rarely write directly about my private life, I recognized these dynamics of silencing. I still remember the years when I could not write the word *I,* even in fiction; the letter at the tip of my pen filled me with terror.

"For my criticism came out of, has always come out of, *enormous feeling*," Zambreno writes, arguing that reading is a bodily experience. "There is nothing objective about the experience of confronting and engaging with and swooning over literature." She argues that taking the "I" out of essays is a form of repression. I don't always use the first person; sometimes I find it clouds rather than enlivens my work. But *Heroines* cut me deeply, and I cannot avoid the "I."

The first time I read the book, I finished it in two days, putting it down only when I was at work. Around this time, I began formulating a new project of my own, imagining the lost voices of women in a particular episode of history. Now I see that it is a reply to the central question of *Heroines:* whose stories are remembered, and whose are erased?

*

I keep circling back to an early passage:

> In Cleveland the local bibliophilic society explicitly prohibits women from joining. John [Zambreno's husband] attended a meeting at the invitation of his colleague at Oberlin. (I was not happy.) One of those quasi-secret societies of rich white men with bizarre rituals, held in some grand Victorian home. The series of tableaux that begin Virginia Woolf's *A Room of One's Own*, her treatise on the material conditions that could allow a woman to write, to write well. Her scenes illuminating women banned from the grounds and libraries and luncheons of the fictional college Oxbridge, to show that a woman of her time would be banned from all the public spaces of reflection and socialization and higher learning that Woolf argues are important in order to begin to have the interior space to roam about in, to think the lucid thoughts that foster Great Texts.

I don't know the specifics of the bibliophilic society, but most of these organizations are outgrowths of an era when women were not allowed to enter the professions or own property and their power derived from their dependence on men. In maintaining this tradition, the bibliophilic society perpetuates the belief that women can at best be dilettantes, never equal to men.

Zambreno juxtaposes this exclusion with the stories of Vivien(ne) Eliot and Zelda Fitzgerald. T.S. Eliot published his wife's satirical sketches of their Bloomsbury society under a pseudonym, but when scandal ensued, he exposed her as the author. This betrayal led to her first breakdown. F. Scott Fitzgerald accusing his wife of stealing his material—their shared life and marriage—in her novel *Save Me the Waltz*. He enlists a psychiatrist to certify her unfit to write, using, among other things, her poor housekeeping as evidence of her insanity.

Why did these men feel threatened by their wives writing? Scott wanted his wife to be his muse, his "complementary intelligence." He freely used her speech and even her diaries as material for his novels.

Writing is a form of power.

In writing *Save Me the Waltz*, Zelda tried to create herself as her own character and take back her power.

Zambreno points out that women like Vivien(ne) and Zelda did not have room to become their own authors. But she also asks: if they hadn't married authoritarian men, would they have become artists? Or would they still have internalized their roles as dilettantes?

*

What about the women who did become writers?

Zambreno describes an adult education class she led. A woman says of Jean Rhys's *Good Morning, Midnight,* a novel on the breakdown of a woman no longer in her prime, "I just feel like Ford Madox Ford [Rhys's patron and sometime lover] put a pen in her hand and said, write your diary dear, we'll just edit it a lot."

Rhys could not have been her own author. A man had to turn her words into art.

Echoing Scott Fitzgerald's dismissal of Zelda's writing as automatic, undisciplined, and diaristic.

This trivialization of the diary form, Zambreno charges, is a covert way of discouraging girls and women from writing:

> The diary especially is read through the context of modernism
> as a form of automatic writing, but worse, of automatic feeling,
> it is the intensity of emotions expressed that seems to render it
> unserious, unliterary, which connects in general to literature by
> women that comes out of the diary form. This is because girls
> write in a diary.

Rhys was dependent on a succession of unreliable lovers and husbands. At her lowest point, she begged old lovers for money. Her fiction depicts the material reality of disempowered women.

I think of Muriel Rukeyser, "What would happen if one woman told the truth about her life? The world would split open."

She could not be her own author. She did not have authority.

Zambreno notes that many literary women, acclaimed and forgotten alike, kept diaries, including Virginia Woolf, Sylvia Plath, Jean Rhys, Anais Nin, Vivien(ne) Eliot, and Zelda Fitzgerald. Their notebooks were integral to their creative processes; they could record their observations, analyze their experiences, and play with ideas without judgment or discipline.

In writing their diaries, they began to roam in their interior spaces.

Heroines is organized as an accretion of fragments that brings to mind a notebook. This form allows her to weave history, criticism, analysis, memoir, and asides into her arguments. The passage on the bibliophilic society I quoted above is exemplar of the form: she begins with a marital dispute, enlarges her lens to a pernicious form of ongoing gender inequity, and references a seminal essay to consider its implications. The conclusions are not always tidy, and as my obsession with this paragraph shows, the ideas remain open to interrogation and interpretation.

This associative style allows Zambreno to reference a wide range of authors and texts and begin building an alternative canon of the girl. "How we buy into this idea of the canon, its memory campaign that verges on propaganda, that the books remembered are the only ones worth reading." In discussing the books she loves and that formed her as a writer, which also include Rhys's *Wide Sargasso Sea*, Djuna Barnes's *Nightwood*, and Jane Bowles's *Two Serious Ladies*, she brings them back into the conversation.

A role of the critic: shaping the discourse on what is worth remembering.

*

Zambreno moves to Akron, Ohio, where John has a position as a rare books librarian. Bored and isolated, she begins a blog, where she connects with a community of women writers. She posts long rants about the mad wives, a subject that has obsessed her for years. Chris Kraus, an editor at Semiotext(e) and author of *I Love Dick*, a novel of a love affair and a performance of abject female subjectivity, contacts Zambreno about turning this work into a book.

Heroines was born of a blog. Zambreno argues that online media such as blogs and Tumblrs are public notebooks in which women and girls can reclaim our stories and write our experiences. Like in the handwritten diaries of the past, we can experiment with ideas and identities. But these reflections are posted in a public space.

A bibliophilic society of sorts. A way to reclaim our authority in the public sphere.

I see the possibilities Zambreno describes. I think of Dodie Bellamy's *the buddhist*, on the aftermath of an affair with a Buddhist teacher. I think of Emily Rapp's *The Still Point of the Turning World*, a chronicle of her infant son's decline from Tay-Sachs, a fatal and incurable genetic disease. Both began as blogs. Online, they could write with immediacy and document a period of their lives, and especially for Rapp, keep friends and family updated when she was too overwhelmed to speak to them in private.

But I also think about why I don't keep a regular blog. I already log many hours in front of the screen. Blogging is also a performance, and like in the physical world, women are expected to conform to certain roles. I don't need the anxiety of constantly monitoring my online persona.

Sometimes withholding is more powerful than disclosure.

I also think of Virginia Woolf in *Street Haunting:*

> As we step out of the house on a fine evening between four and six, we shed the self our friends know us by and become part of that vast republican army of anonymous trampers, whose society is so agreeable after the solitude of one's own room. For there we sit surrounded by objects which perpetually express the oddity of our own temperaments and enforce the memories of our own experience.

The screen can be isolating. After a day in front of it, I want to wander outside.

I also wonder whether, in hiding behind a screen, we are further sequestering ourselves in the home, acquiescing to our cages.

*

It frustrates me that Zambreno conflates women's writing with autobiographical writing about madness. I say this with trepidation, for

Heroines is also an attempt to recover the lost stories of the hysterics. Like Vivien(ne) Eliot, whose papers at the Bodleian Zambreno could not access. The Eliot estate put up a tangle of red tape.

Hysterics are more often romanticized than understood. Their stories written for them.

Think of Dora suffering from aphonia. Freud diagnosed her as having misplaced sexual longings for the man who molested her.

Zelda, the beautiful, flamboyant flapper. She went crazy, sadly. The damaged girl.

There's nothing wrong with you. It's all in your head.

For Zambreno, writing and madness are intertwined. In her early twenties, when she was aspiring but not yet formed as a writer, she had a breakdown and a series of misadventures in psychiatry that decimated her confidence as an artist:

> It cemented something in me, that maybe I wasn't a writer, that maybe I was just fucked-up, still these voices come at me in the dark, when I'm blocked, sometimes even when I'm too productive—what if this is all just word salad? What if I'm just crazy?

She wonders if hysteria is a somatic response to women's limited roles.

She wonders if hysteria is a label for women who transgress their social roles.

(I think of the FEMEN activists who stage topless protests for women's equality, labeled crazy for reclaiming their bodies as their own.)

In writing about the lives and work of the "mad wives," Zambreno is also performing an act of personal exorcism.

But I also see that charges of madness, or in a more surreptitious form, an inadequate grasp on reality, are often leveled at voices, and not necessarily those of hysterics, that threaten the status quo.

In the final paragraphs Zambreno writes,

> If I have communicated anything to you I hope it is the absolute urgency to write yourself, your body, your own experience. The absolute necessity for you to write yourself in order to understand yourself, in order to become yourself. I ask you to fight against your own disappearance. To refuse to self-immolate.

I read this as a challenge to write not just about hysteria but also the truths that shake our complacency. The complexities beneath the gleaming surface.

On Tenacity

I BEGAN READING Louise Glück's poems around the time I handed in the final draft of my first book. Now I can see that the book was a culmination of a decade of work and obsession, but at the time, without the manuscript to anchor my thoughts, I felt adrift. I had to come down from the high of achieving what I had set out to do and had to face the blank page again. For a year, I plunged into another project, until I realized that I was rewriting my first book and that I did not yet have the depth and experience to give the new story the justice it deserves. For another year, I hardly wrote at all. I had a few real-life adventures, but for the most part, I felt that I was waiting at my desk for words that would not arrive. Without my usual way of expressing what I saw and felt, it seemed to me that the world had lost its texture.

During this time, I kept returning to Glück's essay collection, *Proofs and Theories*. The author of sixteen poetry collections and a former US Poet Laureate, among many other honors, Glück writes in these essays that she always felt that when she was not writing, she was unable to write. Each time she finished a book, she fell into a period of "natural silence," during which she did not write at all. This was most acute between her first two books, of which she says:

And it seemed at that time that, in my life, nothing was happening, or nothing with any power to change me ... Nothing I read,
nothing I saw or heard provoked response. And in the absence of
response to the world, the act of writing, which had been, which
is, the center of my life, the act or dream that suffuses life with
meaning, had virtually stopped. For two years I wrote a little,
three or four poems in all, and these seemed no more than tread-
ing water. For two years, I wrote nothing, not a word. It seemed
increasingly impossible to remember a time when I had been fully
alive, impossible to imagine a future in which I would live that
way again.

These intervals of silence, she writes, "require a stoicism very much like
courage; of these, no reader is aware." In these words, I saw a well-regarded
writer coming to terms with her artistic process and her own limitations,
divulging the invisible struggles of the creative life.

Glück's words gave me a way to understand what I was going through
and reassured me that I was not alone in my despair. In the years before
my book came out, I was writing frantically. I remember a week when I
was working late at my job, late enough that the buses had stopped running and I had to take a cab home, and I still wrote into the night, trying
to finish an essay I had promised an editor. Now I see that I was trying to
race against time. I had believed, however irrationally, that there would
be a moment beyond which my voice would be taken away from me and
I would no longer be able to write.

In reading Glück's essays, I also started thinking about ambition,
drive, and tenacity. Ambition is the desire for success. But wanting is not
enough. I have wanted to climb a fourteener—here in Colorado, this is a
peak over 14,000 feet—but I have yet to put in any effort to accomplish
it. And unless I start training for a marathon hike, this will remain an
unrealized ambition. Drive is the will to achieve. It is a state of mind that
propels you to act. In the years before my book came out, I had the drive
to write. I made compromises to have the time and space to make my art.
I did not push myself to climb mountains—I put writing first.

The combination of ambition and drive, along with a lot of luck, can
bring early successes such as a first book. Tenacity, however, is the grit to

keep going when things get rough and, in particular, to get back to the hard, unglamorous work after you taste a modicum of success. In the past couple of years, as I flailed around and tried to find my writing feet again, I wondered, especially in my worst moments, if I should step away from writing and do something else. Now I see that beginnings, with their sense of possibility, are intoxicating. We live in a culture that eschews the long haul in favor of the glitter of the new. It is easier to keep starting again, always dabbling, than it is to commit to a path that leads to places you cannot yet see. I started a couple of new ventures—I call them distraction projects—but I also knew that my life's work lies in writing.

Glück's first book *Firstborn* is not my favorite. In fact, when I read it in her *Collected Poems,* I wondered if I could make it through 600 more pages of suspended sentences, overuse of ellipses, and inflexible manners. On the other hand, I keep going back to her second book *The House on Marshland,* which came out seven years after the first, for inspiration and reassurance that I can stay on this path I have chosen. I cannot speak for Glück's experience, but as a reader, I see that something in her changed in those years of silence and endurance. There are still days when I want to quit, when I want the thrill of outward success over the invisible work, but I am learning to hold on and trust that I can find my way forward.

The Dehumanizing Politics of Likability

WE ARE LIVING in a political and cultural moment increasingly defined by dehumanization. Many of the crimes of our age are predicated on a profound dislike of the other. Whether it is asylum seekers being shuttled into sordid concentration camps, proposals to deny homeless transgender Americans shelter, or "electability" debates raging around women presidential candidates, much of the discrimination and dismissal seems to revolve around the likability/unlikability axis. The vituperative dialogue on social media rages in an environment of anonymity that breeds an inability to treat anyone—likable or not—with civility and respect. Meanwhile, many of us stand by silent, helpless in our discomfort. But this all begs the question: why is likability even relevant?

As a writer and reader, I've long felt that there was something missing from the conversation about likability, whether in fiction or life at large. The issue crystallized for me in 2016 when my first book *Islanders* was published, and I found myself in the curious position of watching a volume of poems about the Angel Island Immigration Station move from "History" to "Current Affairs" as the year went on. In short, none of the Chinese women's poems were preserved as their barracks were damaged in a fire, so I imagined what they might have written on the walls. I also expanded their stories to the husbands and lovers waiting for them in San Francisco, as well as to the staff, both white and Chinese, who were tasked with enforcing the exclusion laws. Not long after the presidential election that year, an interviewer asked me, "In a book like this, some writers would have portrayed these women as angels, but I liked that you didn't do that. Why did you choose to write flawed, messy characters?" This part of our conversation did not make it into print, but I am still thinking about it.

I was not consciously thinking about the likability of my characters when I wrote the book. I wrote them in the only way I knew how, which was to depict them in all their chaotic humanity. I have joked that the book is really about sex, drugs, and violence: men visit brothels as they wait for their wives and children to land. Women long for past trysts as they wait to join the men they were arranged to marry. A cook who helps sneak messages from the Chinese in San Francisco to their loved ones on Angel Island spends his days off at opium dens trying to forget his culpability in this misery. These women, husbands, and lovers betray each other. They keep unforgivable secrets. They are unable to be truly there for one another. They are, in current literary parlance, unlikable characters.

Now I see that I was also trying to depict the effects of trauma and injustice on the individual psyche. One of the central themes of the book is how political decisions can impact our intimate lives. The Chinese exclusion laws first enacted in the late nineteenth century separated families and inflicted pain on immigrants and citizens alike. People subject to such toxic stress tend to act out in ways that hurt the people closest to them; their behavior is far from virtuous, but these are human responses to suffering. And I drew many of the most harrowing stories from the historical record; I could not have made them up if I tried. In one story, a woman attempted to hang herself after her infant son died in custody and her husband's request that she be allowed to attend the boy's funeral in San Francisco was denied by immigration officials, who cited "No unusual hardships found." I wouldn't know how to make any of the people in this story likable.

What is likability anyway? The literary conversation about likable characters has largely focused on whether we read books to make friends and the lack of prestige accorded commercial women's fiction. In 2013,

Claire Messud snapped at a *Publishers Weekly* interviewer who said of the protagonist of her then-newly published novel, *The Woman Upstairs*, "I wouldn't want to be friends with Nora, would you? Her outlook is almost unbearably grim." Messud's response in all its brilliant rage:

> For heaven's sake, what kind of question is that? Would you want to be friends with Humbert Humbert? Would you want to be friends with Mickey Sabbath? Saleem Sinai? Hamlet? Krapp? Oedipus? Oscar Wao? Antigone? Raskolnikov? Any of the characters in *The Corrections*? Any of the characters in *Infinite Jest*? Any of the characters in anything Pynchon has ever written? Or Martin Amis? Or Orhan Pamuk? Or Alice Munro, for that matter? If you're reading to find friends, you're in deep trouble. We read to find life, in all its possibilities. The relevant question isn't "is this a potential friend for me?" but "is this character alive?"

In response, *Good in Bed* novelist Jennifer Weiner pitted the warm and funny female protagonists of chick-lit against the snobbery of literary fiction, arguing in a piece for *Slate* that deriding likable characters is just another way of dismissing women who write commercial fiction. On the other hand, Roxane Gay declared in a 2014 *BuzzFeed* essay that she's "Not Here to Make Friends": women should be allowed to be as bad as they want to be, as ruthless and callous as men. Not long after, the subhead of an article Willa Paskin wrote for *Slate* posed the question, "And if we like an unlikable woman, doesn't that make her likable?" On a *New York Times Book Review* podcast, Messud later clarified, "I couldn't help but feel that it was a gendered question. I don't think we as readers expect to identify with or admire male protagonists, and I suddenly had a feeling that there was this expectation of a woman protagonist by a woman writer."

In many ways, likability *is* a gendered issue. Lacy Johnson writes in her brilliant essay "On Likability," which began as a talk she gave at the 2018 Tin House Summer Workshop, about how she used to acquiesce to men's demands, even at age fourteen, because she "had been taught somewhere along the way that it was a blessing to be liked by a man." Later, she endured an abusive relationship in which she was kidnapped, raped, and almost killed when she tried to leave. Johnson writes, "Stories are how we know ourselves, how we understand our relation to others; stories are the lenses that allow us to look at the chaos of the world and see with clarity and wisdom."

The story she once felt was safe enough to tell was about female obedience. But she began writing a new story for herself, one that put truth above the expectation to please others. "At some point," Johnson writes, "we must acknowledge that the question of likability is not one about craft, but about sexism, racism, homophobia—it's about bigotry." The story that women should be likable—small, compliant, and uncomplaining—is a cage that puts their lives in danger.

The argument over whether we read to make friends reveals a larger problem. That a woman can either be likable and superficial or unlikable and serious is a false dichotomy, but it has taken root in ways that appear natural and inevitable. I am not the first person to notice that the 2016 presidential election was a contest between an unqualified, willfully uninformed man and an exceptionally accomplished woman many branded unlikable, and we have seen how that turned out. (To further underline the double standard: the boorish, raging man in question is, by most people's measure, odious in the extreme.) I am also not the first person to note that, to this day, women who accuse men of sexual assault are shamed for what they wore, how much they drank, or whom they have slept with; their inability to live up to some fantasy of perfect womanhood—their unlikability—is reason to dismiss their credibility. We tell ourselves that we don't have to heed women we label unlikable.

But it is not just women who bear the unreasonable burdens of likability. Now I also see that I did not want to make my characters in *Islanders* "good" victims. The Chinese Exclusion Act was made possible by demagogues who dehumanized the Chinese by saying, in effect, that they were not "good" people. We are in the third year of the presidency of a man who opened his campaign with a pledge to build a wall on the southern border to keep out the "bad hombres." This same man has overseen gross human rights abuses, such as the separation of children from their parents when seeking asylum. At the same time, he is trying to do away with family reunification policies, insisting that we should let in immigrants based on merit only—that is, well-educated, highly employable, and likable. This rhetoric of "good" versus "bad" immigrants still resonates with many Americans, and I did not want to buy into it.

Most of the Chinese women at Angel Island were coming to join their merchant husbands. At the border, they had to undergo extensive interrogations to prove the validity of their relationships. Infidelity, then, was not just a moral failure or an understandable response to trauma; it went against the letter of the law. In portraying my characters—both men and women—at their worst, I was in a way asking, at what point do we deem them no longer deserving of human rights?

Our culture's propensity for rationalizing the stripping away of human dignity—and even human life—by judging a victim unlikable goes well beyond immigration. When Black teenager Michael Brown Jr. was fatally shot by white police officer Darren Wilson in Ferguson, Missouri, in 2014, those defending Wilson leaned heavily on the fact that Brown had just robbed a convenience store. That same year, Alex Nieto, a long-time resident of San Francisco's Bernal Heights, was killed by police after a verbal altercation with a white newcomer to the neighborhood when a bystander thought that Nieto's red 49ers jacket was gang-related and his holstered taser was a firearm. At the wrongful death trial Nieto's parents brought against the police department, the district attorney highlighted Nieto's history of mental illness. When police choked Eric Garner to death in Staten Island in 2014, authorities pointed to his extensive arrest record, much of which entailed minor crimes such as selling untaxed cigarettes and marijuana possession. It is like clockwork: after every incident of police brutality against Black and brown people, the victim is framed as a hoodlum, mentally ill, or, most of all, a criminal, his purported unlikability all the justification needed for, in effect, the death penalty without trial.

The list is long. Beneath all of these stories is the notion that if we are not "good" or "likable" enough, we deserve the injustices perpetrated on us. And by characterizing victims as unlikable or undeserving, we protect the systems of power and privilege that make these atrocities possible in the first place.

I am not saying that we should all write about serial killers who crucify kittens. But likability hinges on respectability, which is another way of saying a "likable" character is one whose presence and portrayal does not make us uncomfortable and does not rock the status quo. When we privilege likability, whether in literature or in life, we limit our emotional range to that which is agreeable and repress the most compassionate parts of ourselves. We fail to see the humanity in people who are unlike us. We disengage from all the rage, trauma, and injustice, embracing a silence that will eventually consume us too.

Notes

HOLLYWOOD PILGRIMS

p. 3   Edward Abbey, *Desert Solitaire* (New York: Touchstone, 1990), 54.

p. 6   *Stagecoach*, directed by John Ford, featuring Claire Trevor and John Wayne (1939; Los Angeles, CA).

COASTLINES

p. 8   Him Mark Lai, Genny Lim, and Judy Yung eds., *Island: Poetry and History of Chinese Immigrants on Angel Island, 1910–1940* (Seattle, University of Washington Press, 1991), 128.

p. 12   Hélène Cixous, "The Laugh of the Medusa," trans. Keith Cohen and Paula Cohen, *Signs* 1, no. 4 (Summer 1976): 880.

p. 13   Lai, et al., 52.

DREAMS OF GOLDEN MOUNTAIN

p. 16   Emma Lazarus, 1883. "The New Colossus," plaque, Statue of Liberty, New York City.

p. 16   Lai, et al., 54.

p. 19   Wong Chin Foo, "Why Am I a Heathen?," *North American Review* 145, no. 369 (August 1887): 169–179.

p. 20   Scott D. Seligman, *The First Chinese American: The Remarkable Life of Wong Chin Foo* (Hong Kong: Hong Kong University Press, 2013), ix.

p. 21   Seligman, 116.

p. 21   Seligman, 80.

FIRECRACKER

p. 24   Rebecca Solnit, *The Encyclopedia of Trouble and Spaciousness* (San Antonio, TX: Trinity University Press, 2014), 245.

AT THE RUINS

p. 28   J. B. Jackson, *A Sense of Place, A Sense of Time* (New Haven, CT: Yale University Press, 1994), 23.

WESTERN JOURNEYS

p. 33   Bernard DeVoto, *The Year of Decision* (New York: St. Martin's Griffin, 2000), 164.

p. 33   Zebulon Pike, Appendix to Part II, *An Account of the Expeditions to the Sources of the Mississippi and through the Western Parts of Louisiana to the Sources of the Arkansaw, Kans, La Platte, and Pierre Jaun, Rivers* (Philadelphia: C. & A. Conrad, 1810), 8. https://content .wisconsinhistory.org/digital/collection/aj/id/12745

p. 33   Richard H. Dillon, "Stephen Long's Great American Desert," *Proceedings of the American Philosophical Society* 111, no. 2 (April 14, 1967): 102.

p. 34   Charles Dana Wilbur, *The Great Valleys and Prairies of Nebraska and the Northwest* (Omaha: Daily Republican Printing, 1881).

p. 35   Isabella Bird, *A Lady's Life in the Rocky Mountains* (Norman: University of Oklahoma Press, 1960), 136.

p. 35   Bird, 138.

p. 36   Jack Kerouac, *On the Road* (New York: Penguin, 1976), 32.

p. 37   Louise C. Harrison, *Empire and the Berthoud Pass* (Denver: Big Mountain Press, 1974).

p. 38   Hop Alley/Chinese Riot of 1880, plaque, lower downtown Denver, 20th and Blake streets.[*]

p. 39   William Wei, *Asians in Colorado: A History of Persecution and Perseverance in the Centennial State* (Seattle: University of Washington Press, 2016), 208.

p. 40   Ralph Carr Memorial, 1976, statue, Sakura Square, Denver.

p. 40   Special Correspondent. "The Kansas Pacific Railroad," *New York Times*, September 12, 1870.

---

[*] On August 8, 2022 this plaque was removed in an effort to more accurately represent the Hop Alley incident and the experiences of the Chinese community members who were victims of this anti-Chinese race riot. See https://www.rmpbs.org/blogs/news/denver-removes-anti -chinese-historical-plaque/.

ASCENT

p. 44 John Denver, vocalist. "Rocky Mountain High." By John Denver and Mike Taylor. Recorded August 1972. Track 1 on *Rocky Mountain High*. RCA Records.

p. 44 Joan Didion, *Where I Was From* (New York: Vintage, 2003), 74.

p. 47 William N. Byers, "The First Recorded Ascent of Long's Peak," *Rocky Mountain News,* September 1, 1868.

p. 48 Bird, 94.

p. 48 Bird, 101.

THE IDEOLOGY OF PARADISE

p. 53 "It Started with a Family," Stanford 125, https://125.stanford.edu/kiosk /k01/.

p. 54 Memorial Church inscription, Stanford University campus, North Wall of the Nave.

A MEMORY OF HILLS

p. 59 David Mason, *Ludlow* (Los Angeles: Red Hen Press, 2007), 78.

p. 60 Mason, 70.

p. 60 Mason, 85.

p. 61 Mason, 221.

AT THE PONDS

p. 63 Claudia Toburen, Appendix A: *A Nature Area for Boulder County: A Pilot Surface Mining Project.* Resources Development Internship Program, Western Interstate Commission for Higher Education, 1974, in *Walden Ponds Wildlife Habitat Management Plan*, August 31, 2010. https://assets.bouldercounty.gov/wp-content/uploads/2017/03 /walden-ponds-management-plan.pdf.

p. 64 Clayborne Carson, ed. *The Autobiography of Martin Luther King Jr.* (New York: Warner Books, 1998), 14.

p. 65 Henry David Thoreau, *Walden; or, Life in the Woods,* (London: J. M. Dent, 1908), 201.

THE ROAD HOME

p. 72 Kirk Johnson, "Note to Christo: Don't Start Hanging Fabric Yet," *New York Times*, February 1, 2012, https://www.nytimes.com/2012/02/02/us /christo-over-the-river-project-divides-coloradans.html.

p. 74 *Christo and Jeanne-Claude: Over the River* (Cologne, Germany: Taschen, 2008).

p. 77   Randy Kennedy, "Christo, Trump, and the Art World's Biggest Protest Yet," *New York Times*, January 25, 2017, https://www.nytimes.com/2017 /01/25/arts/design/christo-protest-donald-trump-colorado-artwork .html.

FLOWERS OF PRISON

p. 81   Carol Strickland, "Ai Weiwei Breaks Into Alcatraz," *Art in America*, October 8, 2014, https://www.artnews.com/art-in-america/features/ai -weiwei-breaks-into-alcatraz-59856/.

p. 85   Tim Lewis, "Ai Weiwei: 'An Artist Must Be an Activist,'" *Guardian*, March 22, 2020, https://www.theguardian.com/artanddesign/2020 /mar/22/ai-weiwei-an-artist-must-be-an-activist.

SPLIT

p. 87   Peter Sloterdijk, *Terror From the Air*, trans. by Amy Patton and Steve Corcoran (Los Angeles: Semiotext(e), 2009), 25.

p. 87   Sloterdijk, 22–23.

p. 88   Interview with Allison Smith, in *Allison Smith: Needle Work*, text by Wendy Vogel, et al. (St. Louis: Mildred Lane Kemper Art Museum, Washington University in St. Louis, 2010), 39.

FOOTSTEPS ON THE SEA

p. 92   Rebecca Solnit, *Storming the Gates of Paradise: Landscapes for Politics* (Berkeley: University of California Press, 2007), 1.

p. 92   Solnit, 310.

p. 93   Solnit, 21.

p. 96   Delphine Hirasuna, preface to Gardens of Alcatraz, by John Hart, Russell A. Beatty, and Michael Boland, with photographs by Roy Eisenhardt (San Francisco: Golden Gate National Parks Association, 1996).

p. 97   Elliott Michener, "The Gardens of Alcatraz," The Golden Gate National Park Conservancy, https://www.alcatrazgardens.org/elliott-michener .php.

p. 97   Lai, et al., 34.

REFUGE

p. 110   Xandra McMahon, "As Rocky Flats Refuge Opening Nears, Former Workers, Opponents Still Harbor Doubts," *Colorado Public Radio News*, May 15, 2018, https://www.cpr.org/2018/05/15/as-rocky-flats -refuge-opening-nears-former-workers-opponents-still-harbor-doubts/.

THE GHOSTS OF BITTER CREEK

p. 120   A. Dudley Gardner, "The Chinese in Wyoming: Life in the Core and Peripheral Communities," *South Dakota History*, 33, no. 4 (Winter 2003): 389–390, https://www.sdhspress.com/journal/south -dakota-history-33-4/the-chinese-in-wyoming-life-in-the-core -and-peripheral-communities/vol-33-no-4-the-chinese-in-wyoming .pdf.

HOME LANDS

p. 126   Eduardo Galeano, *Open Veins of Latin America*, translated by Cedric Belfrage (New York: Monthly Review Press, 1997), 266.

THE STORIES THAT BIND US

p. 143   Poe Ballantine, *Love and Terror on the Howling Plains of Nowhere* (Portland, OR: Hawthorne Books, 2013), 84.

p. 143   Joan Didion, *The White Album*, (New York: Simon & Schuster, 1979), 11.

p. 144   Ballantine, 19.

p. 145   Ballantine, 139.

THE SUBJECTIVE PASSIONS

p. 150   Veronica Gonzalez Peña, *The Sad Passions* (Los Angeles: Semiotext(e), 2013), 11.

p. 151   Gonzalez Peña, 332.

p. 152   Gonzalez Peña, 334.

p. 152   Gonzalez Peña, 338.

LOST AND FOUND

p. 154   Kate Zambreno, *Heroines* (Los Angeles: Semiotext(e), 2012), 280.

p. 154   Zambreno, 19.

p. 156   Zambreno, 276.

p. 156   Muriel Rukeyser, "Kathe Kollwitz," in *The Collected Poems of Muriel Rukeyser*, ed. Janet E. Kaufman & Anne F. Herzog (Pittsburgh: University of Pittsburg Press, 2005), 463.

p. 157   Zambreno, 264.

p. 158   Virginia Woolf, "Street Haunting." *The Death of the Moth and Other Essays* (New York: Harcourt Brace, 1942), 20–21.

p. 159   Zambreno, 254.

p. 160   Zambreno, 296.

ON TENACITY

p. 162   Louise Glück, *Proofs and Theories: Essays on Poetry* (New Jersey: Ecco, 1994), 132.

p. 162   Glück, 27.

THE DEHUMANIZING POLITICS OF LIKABILITY

p. 166   Claire Messud, "An Unseemly Emotion: PW Talks with Claire Messud," interview by Annasue McCleave Wilson, *Publishers Weekly,* April 29, 2013.

p. 166   Jennifer Weiner, "I Like Likable Characters," *Slate*, May 22, 2013.

p. 166   Roxane Gay, "Not Here to Make Friends," *Buzzfeed*, January 3, 2014.

p. 166   Willa Paskin, "What's So Bad About Likable Women?," *Slate*, January 10, 2014.

p. 166   Pamela Paul, "Book Review Podcast: Claire Messud and More," May 13, 2013, *New York Times* Book Review podcast, 38:59, https://www.nytimes.com/audio/2013/05/03/books/review/05books_pod.html.

p. 167   Lacy Johnson, "On Likability." *Tin House,* October 11, 2018.

Bibliography

ESSAYS AND MEMOIR

Abbey, Edward. *Desert Solitaire*. New York: Touchstone, 1990.

Ballantine, Poe. *Love and Terror on the Howling Plains of Nowhere*. Portland, OR: Hawthorne Books, 2013.

Bird, Isabella. *A Lady's Life in the Rocky Mountains*. Norman: University of Oklahoma Press, 1960.

Cassady, Neal. *The First Third*. San Francisco: City Lights Publishers, 2001.

Cixous, Hélène. "The Laugh of the Medusa." Translated by Keith Cohen and Paula Cohen. *Signs* 1, no. 4 (Summer 1976): 875–893.

Didion, Joan. *Slouching Towards Bethlehem*. New York: Farrar, Straus & Giroux, 2008.

Didion, Joan. *Where I Was From*. New York: Vintage, 2003.

Didion, Joan. *The White Album*. New York: Simon & Schuster, 1979.

Foo, Wong Chin. "Why Am I a Heathen?" *North American Review* 145, no. 369 (August 1887): 169–179.

Glück, Louise. *Proofs and Theories: Essays on Poetry*. New Jersey: Ecco, 1994.

Hirasuna, Delphine. Preface to *Gardens of Alcatraz*, by John Hart, Russell A. Beatty, and Michael Boland, with photographs by Roy Eisenhardt. San Francisco: Golden Gate National Parks Association, 1996.

Jackson, J. B. *A Sense of Place, a Sense of Time*. New Haven, CT: Yale University Press, 1994.

Powell, John Wesley. *The Exploration of the Colorado River and Its Canyons*. New York: Penguin Books, 1987.

Solnit, Rebecca. *Encyclopedia of Trouble and Spaciousness*. San Antonio: Trinity University Press, 2014.

Solnit, Rebecca. *Storming the Gates of Paradise: Landscapes for Politics*. Berkeley: University of California Press, 2007.

Thoreau, Henry David. *Civil Disobedience and Other Essays*. New York: Dover Publications, 1993.

Thoreau, Henry David. *Walden, or, Life in the Woods*. London: J. M. Dent, 1908.

Woolf, Virginia. *A Room of One's Own*. Orlando, FL: Harcourt Brace, 1991.

Woolf, Virginia. "Street Haunting." In *The Death of the Moth and Other Essays*. 20–21. New York: Harcourt Brace, 1942.

HISTORY AND BIOGRAPHY

Carson, Clayborne, ed. *The Autobiography of Martin Luther King Jr.* New York: Warner Books, 1998.

Chang, Gordon H. *Ghosts of Gold Mountain: The Epic Story of the Chinese Who Built the Transcontinental Railroad*. New York: Houghton Mifflin Harcourt, 2019.

Childs, Craig. *House of Rain: Tracking a Vanished Civilization Across the American Southwest*. New York: Little, Brown, 2007.

DeVoto, Bernard. *The Year of Decision*. New York: St. Martin's Griffin, 2000.

Golden Gate National Park Conservancy. "Elliott Michener." The Gardens of Alcatraz (website). https://www.alcatrazgardens.org/elliott-michener.php.

Harrison, Louise C. *Empire and the Berthoud Pass*. Denver: Big Mountain Press, 1974.

Isham, Dell. *Rock Springs Massacre 1885*. Fort Collins: self-published, 1985.

Lai, Him Mark, Genny Lim, and Judy Yung, eds. *Island: Poetry and History of Chinese Immigrants on Angel Island, 1910–1940*. 2nd ed. Seattle: University of Washington Press, 2014.

Lee, Erika. *The Making of Asian America*. New York: Simon & Schuster, 2015.

Lee, Erika, and Judy Yung. *Angel Island: Immigrant Gateway to America*. Oxford: Oxford University Press, 2010.

Limerick, Patricia Nelson. *The Legacy of Conquest*. New York: W.W. Norton & Company, 1987.

MacDonald, Dougald. *Longs Peak: The Story of Colorado's Favorite Fourteener*. Englewood, CO: Westcliffe Publishers, 2004.

Pike, Zebulon. *An Account of the Expeditions to the Sources of the Mississippi and through the Western Parts of Louisiana to the Sources of the Arkansaw, Kans, La Platte, and Pierre Jaun,* Rivers. Philadelphia: C. & A. Conrad, 1810.

Rudolph, Gerald E. "The Chinese in Colorado, 1869–1911." Master's Thesis, University of Denver, 1964.

Schivelbusch, Wolfgang. *Railway Journey: The Industrialization of Time and Space in the 19th Century*. Berkeley: University of California Press, 1986.

Seligman, Scott D. *The First Chinese American: The Remarkable Life of Wong Chin Foo*. Hong Kong: Hong Kong University Press, 2013.

Stegner, Wallace. *Beyond the Hundredth Meridian: John Wesley Powell and the Second Opening of the West*. New York: Penguin Books, 1992.

Storti, Craig. *Incident at Bitter Creek: The Story of the Rock Springs Chinese Massacre*. Ames: Iowa State University Press, 1991.[1*]

Toburen, Claudia. Appendix A: *A Nature Area for Boulder County: A Pilot Surface Mining Project*. Resources Development Internship Program, Western Interstate Commission for Higher Education, 1974. In *Walden Ponds Wildlife Habitat Management Plan*, August 31, 2010. https://assets.bouldercounty.gov/wp-content/uploads/2017/03/walden-ponds-management-plan.pdf.

Wei, William. *Asians in Colorado: A History of Persecution and Perseverance in the Centennial State*. Seattle: University of Washington Press, 2016.

White, Richard. *Railroaded: The Transcontinentals and the Making of Modern America*. New York: W.W. Norton, 2011.

Wilbur, Charles Dana. *The Great Valleys and Prairies of Nebraska and the Northwest*. Omaha: Daily Republican Printing Company, 1881.

CRITICISM

Boetzkes, Amanda. *The Ethics of Earth Art*. Minneapolis: University of Minnesota Press, 2010.

Deutsche, Rosalyn. *Evictions: Art and Spatial Politics*. Boston: MIT Press, 1996.

Galeano, Eduardo. *Open Veins of Latin America*. Translated by Cedric Belfrage. New York: Monthly Review Press, 1997.

Lippard, Lucy. *The Lure of the Local: Senses of Place in a Multicentered Society*. New York: New Press, 1997.

Sloterdijk, Peter. *Terror From the Air*. Translated by Amy Patton and Steve Corcoran. Los Angeles: Semiotext(e), 2009.

Zambreno, Kate. *Heroines*. Los Angeles: Semiotext(e), 2012.

FICTION

Diaz, Junot. *The Brief Wondrous Life of Oscar Wao*. New York: Penguin, 2007.

Gonzalez Peña, Veronica. *The Sad Passions*. Los Angeles: Semiotext(e), 2013.

Kerouac, Jack. *On the Road*. New York: Penguin, 1976.

---

* Storti's book is the only comprehensive history of the massacre currently available. It is well researched, but it has issues: he claims that the Rock Springs Massacre and the Chinese Exclusion Act have "little to do with race prejudice or immigration policy. The issue, rather, was the status of the American workingman in the industrial era."

POETRY

Glück, Louise. *Poems 1962–2012*. New York: Farrar, Straus and Giroux, 2012.

Lazarus, Emma. "The New Colossus." 1883. Plaque, Statue of Liberty. New York City.

Mason, David. *Ludlow*. Los Angeles: Red Hen Press, 2007.

Rukeyser, Muriel. "Kathe Kollwitz." In *The Collected Poems of Muriel Rukeyser*, edited by Janet E. Kaufman and Anne F. Herzog, 460–464. Pittsburg: University of Pittsburg Press, 2005.

Snyder, Gary. *Mountains and Rivers Without End*. Berkeley: Counterpoint, 1996.

ART CATALOG

Allison Smith: Needle Work. Text by Wendy Vogel et al. Mildred Lane Kemper Art Museum, Washington University in St. Louis, 2010.

Christo and Jeanne-Claude: Over the River. Text by Jonathan Fineberg et al. Cologne, Germany, Taschen, 2008.

ARTICLES

Byers, William N. "The First Recorded Ascent of Long's Peak." *Rocky Mountain News,* September 1, 1868.

Dillon, Richard H. "Stephen Long's Great American Desert." *Proceedings of the American Philosophical Society* 111, no. 2 (April 14, 1967): 93–108.

Gardner, A. Dudley. "The Chinese in Wyoming: Life in the Core and Peripheral Communities." *South Dakota History* 33, no.2 (Winter 2003):380–390.

Gay, Roxane. "Not Here To Make Friends." *Buzzfeed*, January 3, 2014.

Johnson, Kirk. "Note to Christo: Don't Start Hanging Fabric Yet." *New York Times*, February 1, 2012.

Johnson, Lacy. "On Likability." *Tin House*, October 11, 2018.

Kennedy, Randy. "Christo, Trump, and the Art World's Biggest Protest Yet." *New York Times*, January 25, 2017.

Lewis, Tim. "Ai Weiwei: 'An Artist Must Be an Activist.'" *Guardian*, March 22, 2020.

McMahon, Xandra. "As Rocky Flats Refuge Opening Nears, Former Workers, Opponents Still Harbor Doubts." *Colorado Public Radio News*, May 15, 2018.

Paul, Pamela. "Book Review Podcast: Claire Messud and More." May 13, 2013. *New York Times* Book Review podcast, 38.59. https://www.nytimes.com/audio/2013/05/03/books/review/05books_pod.html.

Paskin, Willa. "What's So Bad About Likable Women?" *Slate*, January 10, 2014.

Solnit, Rebecca. "We Won't Bow Down." *Nation*, March 1, 2010.

Special Correspondent. "The Kansas Pacific Railroad," *The New York Times*, September 12, 1870.

Strickland, Carol. "Ai Weiwei Breaks Into Alcatraz." *Art in America*, October 8, 2014.

Weiner, Jennifer. "I Like Likable Characters." *Slate*, May 22, 2013.

Wilson, Annasue McCleave. "An Unseemly Emotion: PW Talks with Claire Messud." *Publishers Weekly*, April 29, 2013.

FILM

Ford, John, dir. *Stagecoach*. 1939; Los Angeles, CA: Walter Wanger Productions.